MANAGING
PUBLIC ORGANIZATION
THROUGH LEADERSHIP

NAPOLEON IMARHIAGBE, Ph.D.

authorHOUSE®

AuthorHouse™
1663 Liberty Drive
Bloomington, IN 47403
www.authorhouse.com
Phone: 1 (800) 839-8640

Published by AuthorHouse   09/09/2015

ISBN: 978-1-5049-2336-1 (sc)
ISBN: 978-1-5049-2335-4 (e)

Library of Congress Control Number: 2015911410

Print information available on the last page.

Any people depicted in stock imagery provided by Thinkstock are models, and such images are being used for illustrative purposes only. Certain stock imagery © Thinkstock.

This book is printed on acid-free paper.

CONTENTS

CHAPTER 1: BREADTH COMPONENT   **1**

INTRODUCTION   1

Leadership for Public Organizations   3

Different Types of Leadership Styles   6

Decision Making and Leadership Styles   8

Leadership and Surveys   9

Leadership and Organization Performance   11

Performance Evaluation and Data   11

Organization Performance and Employees' Ideas   17

Training and Performance   18

Recommendations   21

CONCLUSION   22

REFERENCES   25

CHAPTER 2: DEPTH COMPONENT   **27**

INTRODUCTION   27

Organizational Change in Different Sectors   28

Reasons for Organizational Change   29

Managing Organizational Change   31

Leadership and Resistance to Change   34

Overcoming Resistance to Change and Leadership   38

Leadership Models for Managing Change   40

Recommendations   42

CONCLUSION   43

ANNOTATED BIBLIOGRAPHY   46

REFERENCES   55

CHAPTER 3: APPLICATION COMPONENT   59

INTRODUCTION   59

Public Bureaucracy and Social Service Organizations   61

Decision-Making Power and Public-Organization Leaders   65

Bureaucracy and the Personnel System   68

Recommendations   70

CONCLUSION   71

REFERENCES   74

GLOSSARY   77

I would like to dedicate this book to the Walden University Advanced Knowledge Area Module Number V for its leadership and commitment in training PhD students to become expert in Public Management.

ACKNOWLEDGMENTS

First of all, I want to thank the almighty God for keeping me alive, so that I might have the opportunity to complete this book. As I understand it, everyone has a purpose to serve in life, and one of the greater opportunities for purposeful action is to write a book that potentially improves the well-being of others. A book aimed at improving government services or social services is a part of that greater purpose, a researcher's achievement in life.

It would give me great pressure to show my gratitude to AuthorHouse Publishers for making this book possible. Special thanks to Editide' editors for their propositions, remarks, understanding, and patience. They did a remarkable job. It would also be honor to express gratitude to my late parents, Lawrence Imarhiagbe and Agnes Imarhiagbe, my sisters and my brothers for their endless support in my life and allowing me to make all my decisions.

I would also like to thank my wife and children for their unconditional love and sacrifices for me. Thanks also to my former Professor and Mentor, the Dean of Business Administration at Medgar Evars College (CUNY), Dr. John Flateau, for inspiring me to pursue a doctorate degree in Public Policy and Administration. I would also like to take the opportunity to show appreciation to my co-workers, for their expert cooperation on every occasion. I would like to recognize my co-worker and friend, a creative writer, Maxcine Worrell for her boundless support. I am also like to be grateful to the Faculty of the School of Public Policy and Administration at Walden University, especially my former dissertation mentor, Dr. Sally Thomason, and my former dissertation chair, Dr. David W. Hays for their

Napoleon Imarhiagbe, Ph.D.

contributions to this book and the role they played in my KAM research project. I would also like to recognize my friend, Dominic Ekeigwe, MPA, MSW, a practicing politician and a public administrator for his interest in Nigeria's Government politics.

TRADEMARKS AND RIGHTS

Throughout this book, we refer to products and designs which are not our property. These references are meant only to be informational. We do not represent the companies mentioned and were not paid promotional fees. However, if these companies would like to send us evaluation copies of future products, we would be thrilled. References to products are not endorsements, but reflect our opinions in some cases.

Computer software products mentioned are the property of their respective publishers. Instead of attempting to list every software publisher and brand, or including trademark symbols throughout this book, we assume that you know these product and brand names are protected under U.S. and international laws. Fonts and designs are the intellectual property of the design artists. Although U.S. copyright laws do not protect font designs, we consider them the property of the designers and licensing agencies.

INTRODUCTION TO THE BOOK'S ORGANIZATION

Chapter 1 Breadth Component

Chapter 2 Depth Component

Chapter 3 Application Component

PREFACE

This book is a version of the Walden University's unit of study: the Breadth, Depth, and Application components of the advanced Knowledge Area Module (KAM) V. KAM V is one of the required research projects in the School of Management for students completing their PhD in Public Policy and Administration. The university uses this research project to train students to become expert in public management.

Chapter 1, the Breadth Component, explores the problems of public bureaucracy and explicates how public leaders can reform the system. It also explains the weaknesses in public organizations and how they affect the performance of workers. This chapter also addresses different types of leadership styles: fact based, creativity based, feelings based, and power based. The effective-communication skills described in the Breadth section examine other researchers' work, and use their arguments to make an important contribution to the study. Indeed, the communication skills demonstrated in the Breadth Component are by considering other researchers' arguments to make intelligent and valid judgment in the study. This section shows the intellectual capability of using good communication skills to improve the work and job performance of public managers. The chapter includes recommendations and conclusions about how public managers make decisions using different types of leadership styles, which are essential in reducing performance deficits and bringing effective reform to public organizations.

Chapter 2, the Depth Component, examines how public leaders can develop strategies to manage and overcome workers' resistance to change. The reasons for workers' resistance to change are illustrated. The key concept of the Depth Component is to find ways for leaders to respond to and manage organizational change. In this chapter, it also describes how leaders' ideas can reform the way public organizations do business to bring better change to the public system. In addition, this chapter demonstrates different kinds of leadership models for managing change and elucidates how public leaders can use transformational, transactional, developmental, and transitional models to overcome workers' resistance to organizational change. The chapter ends with recommendations, conclusions, and an annotated bibliography.

Chapter 3, the application component, identifies the hindrances that come with a traditional bureaucracy, such as poor delivery of services, lack of resources, flexibility, and innovation. In this chapter, I pay special attention to how bureaucratic systems affect leaders who run social organizations. I also examine other bureaucratic problems facing welfare agencies: slowdown in work processes, and rapid changes in policies and procedures. The most important social issue covered in this chapter is identifying the problems of public bureaucracy and its inability to improve workers' performance. The key weakness of public leaders is attributed to low job performance, poor managerial approaches in the delivery of public services, and lack of innovation. The chapter includes several examples of how public leaders can manage problems that arise in traditional public bureaucracies. This chapter ends with recommendations and conclusions.

CHAPTER 1

BREADTH COMPONENT

Introduction

Governments conduct business through a maze of bureaucracies. The size of public bureaucracy has increased significantly over the past 3 decades (Stillman, 1996). As public bureaucracies continue to grow, red tape and hierarchies have become too difficult to manage. Hence, the need to reform public management is necessary to cut through red tape and bureaucratic redundancy. Researchers showed that work ethics have declined in public management because of its bureaucratic, hierarchical structure (Kobrak, 2002). Managing these public organizations requires leaders with the right vision to rectify these problems and introduce new approaches that will not only reform public management, but also surpass private and nonprofit organizations in how management operates. Consequently, this book vigorously explores how the right leadership can reform and transform public management.

Indeed, the transformation of public organizations cannot take place without the reform of public bureaucracy. The reform of traditional public bureaucracy is necessary because the system is ineffective, and can no longer survive in today's work environment. The problem that comes with traditional bureaucracy is far greater than what most researchers anticipated (Smith, 1997). Bureaucracy slows down the work process, and it is one hindrance to an effective delivery of public services.

Anechiarico and Jacobs (1996) supported the notion that "slowness and delay are pervasive and serious failings of bureaucracy. Practically anyone who has had experience with large-scale bureaucratic government knows this very well. For many people, government is hopelessly slow, unwieldy, inefficient, and bureaucratic" (p. 174). Public bureaucracy has damaged the morality and motivation of workers. Employees in public organizations have been distrustful and unhappy about the bureaucratic-management system (Anechiarico & Jacobs, 1996).

The Smith (1997) study supported the notion:

> Bureaucracy affects peoples' thinking. It becomes a top-down mental attitude approach of doing business. This bureaucratic attitude is harmful, and it can become a debilitating disease. It limits peoples' ideas and innate potential. It can rob pride from people, treating workers as if they are incapable of thinking and unable to make decisions. (p. 56)

In this regard, one can also argue that bureaucracy is a caste system. The hierarchy system restricts workers' ability to perform their tasks. Smith (1997) demonstrated that the work process in public bureaucracy is slow because the responsibility and power to make decisions is removed from employees who need it most. "The traditional bureaucracy has a top-down decision-making process. Ideas, projects, and decisions must push up the chain of command for approval; if approved, the decision finally cascades back down for action" (pp. 57–58). Consequently, this process hampers workers' day-to-day activities.

What is more important is that public bureaucracy is more complicated because it rests on rules and regulations that govern public management. Workers are compelled to follow multiple standards and procedures. As a result, they devote less time to the actual work they do. Behn (2004) explicated, "Government agencies are particularly prone to this kind of performance failure. After all, public employees are required to follow so many processes that devotion to these processes often displaces their commitment to results" (p. 10). Changing public bureaucracy is not going to be an easy task for any leader. That is why public organizations need more than ordinary managers to address the complexity of public bureaucracy. Public organizations should search for new leaders with the capacity to change traditional bureaucratic structures, which have been the main obstacles to workers' productivity. These new leaders must be competent and have the skills to inspire the workforce to be more productive (Milakovich & Gordon, 2001).

Leadership for Public Organizations

The ideal leader in U.S. public administration has the vision and values to introduce new changes that have a huge impact on workers. The vision of any leader, whether in public or private organizations, is to implement ideas and methodologies to achieve the organization's goals. Leaders judge the effectiveness of the policies they apply (Maccoby, 1983). History also has shown that the progress of an organization depends on the quality of the leader. Good leadership brings stability and creates pathways for development (Syett, 1992). Specifically, "a leader is a person who is effective in achieving worthy results, in any field, and no matter what the obstacles, with unfailing regard for human beings" (Koestenbaum,1991, p 316). In fact, leaders must be able to find solutions and accomplish any task, no matter the difficulty. Leaders can be found in every walk of life. Leaders tend to inspire people and lead others by setting examples. They do not have separate sets of genes nor are they in any way superior to any other human, physically or mentally. However, they tend to possess those characteristics that make them a leader.

In addition, leaders should be able to take the road others have not taken before. To change from the old ways to new ones, new styles of leadership are required to create strategies that enable the organization move in new directions and arrive at expected destinations (Smith, 1997). Shafritz and Russell (2005, p. 365) affirmed that "the job of the leader of any organization is to get people to do things they have never done before, to do things that are not routine, and to take risks and sometimes even to die for the common good." However, leaders are those who do not always introduce new ideas; they are also willing to support others' views to find a solution to the problem at hand. Good leaders try to learn from their mistakes, and they do not always take credit for their work (Angelucci, 2005).

Importantly, the duty of a leader is to get workers to commit to the philosophy of the organization. It is also the responsibility of a leader to lead and direct the organization to produce its optimal output. Thus, leaders must be able to empower workers. Leaders not only produce detailed plans, but also provide ideas for their organizations and strategies to accomplish their goals. Public-management leaders must be able to demonstrate their organizations' goals and motivate workers to achieve them (Kobrak, 2002). Leaders must be able to explain to workers why their organizations need changes and how these changes will be implemented. New public-organization leaders must be able to master all aspects of the job. They should be able to gain the respect of the workers by demonstrating that they know the job. More importantly, leaders should demonstrate that they are competent, because an organization without competent leaders is likely to fail. Macbeth became an incompetent leader because he lost the respect and admiration of his followers. As a result, his organization was doomed, as he was (Shafritz & Russell, 2005).

Leadership is an instrument to reform public management. Public administrators are eager for quality leaders to meet the challenge of reform in the public sector. More importantly, public-management policies vary, and without someone with good leadership skills to interpret and implement them, workers will be diverting from their goals. Public management is a form of institution that cannot run without a leader to set aims and strategies for employees to follow.

Indeed, leaders in public organizations are essential for the organization because, without them, it will be very difficult to deal with complex policy issues (Kobrak, 2002). Leadership from public managers is essential because organizations need someone with the managerial skills, knowledge, and expertise required to manage public organizations. Additionally, public organizations are very difficult to operate because of inadequate resources. Elected chief executives provide public managers with few materials and workers to handle massive public-organization resources. Kobrak (2002) illustrated:

Leadership from public manager is necessary because the legislative branch of government gives public agencies missions that are vague and conflicting and often fails to provide enough resources to pursue seriously all these missions.... Leadership from public mangers is necessary because the judiciary, which is charged with overseeing the constitutionality and legality of activities of public agencies and public mangers, often focuses on narrow issues of process rather than the broader concerns of achieving public purposes. (p. 50)

Hence, having leadership in public organizations is quite as necessary as the need for a doctor in a medical clinic, because having medicines in a clinic will not cure patients but a doctor's prescription will (Kobrak, 2002). Similarly, having a legislative office and developing certain policies does not entail smooth accomplishment of tasks and vision set out by government; rather, dedicated leaders are not only energetic and enthusiastic, but patriotic and dedicated to their task.

Additionally, public-organization leaders are responsible for the interpretation and implementation of vague public policy. U.S. public administration certainly does not function perfectly, but using various effective leadership skills, public managers can resolve some complications that come with public bureaucracy. Indeed, by introducing good leadership skills, leaders can strengthen public organizations and make them more effective.

Governmental policy needs more than a public manager to address the complexity that comes with public management. Public organizations need not only managers with managerial skills, but also leaders who are creative, with visions about how to transform public organizations. Transforming government organizations should rely on leaders with the potential to change the traditional bureaucratic structures that hamper public management (Haff, 2003). In fact, public organizations need leaders to make the changes that will transform the bureaucratic, hierarchical structure to a well-organized functioning workforce.

These leaders must be visionaries, and they must be creative and have the management skills to ensure that the changes implemented are materialized and effective. Undoubtedly, traditional bureaucratic administrative structures cannot be easily changed. To enact change, new public-management leaders must put more energy and resources in removing the barriers and hindrances that have occurred through years of bureaucratic management. New public-organization leaders must have the intellectual capacity to bring public management out of bureaucratic disorder (Shafritz & Russell, 2005). They must be able to recognize public organizations and transform them to workforces that are more productive.

To transform public bureaucracy, new leaders should exercise authority or power (Shafritz & Russell, 2005). More importantly, public-organization leaders should not sit at the top of the hierarchy and direct others. New public-management leaders accomplish goals by carefully analyzing every aspect of the organization. They can list all management problems and use scorecards to analyze these issues. These new leaders learn to look at the history of similar problems and identify how they occurred. In addition, they know how to analyze different experts' ideas and choose the best ones to resolve problems. A confident public-management leader can set a timetable for when organizational goals will be achieved.

Different Types of Leadership Styles

Many leaders use their authority in different ways to run their organizations. Some leaders like to give orders to subordinates and punish those who do not follow their instructions. Some leaders like to show that they are expert in their professions. They never disappoint when they are supposed to perform difficult tasks. Leaders may believe in persuasion as the most important part of their authority or power. Whatever preference inspired leaders, they like to use the leadership style that is comfortable for them.

Shafritz and Russell, (2005) illustrated five types of leadership styles that may be suitable for public-management leaders: expert, referent, reward, legitimate, and coercive:

- Type 1 (Expert power): Power is based on expert knowledge. Leaders with expert power not only set direction for workers to follow, but also know how well the job is being performed. Furthermore, such leaders can be known as think tanks because of their unique ability to engage innovative and creative methods to derive solutions. This is only possible because of their command over knowledge. Simply, they are jacks-of-all-trades in knowledge acquisition.

- Type 2 (Referent power): Leadership power is based on how followers perceive their leader's personality. Workers admire their leaders not because of their expertise but because of their personalities. Such types of leaders are the charmers: those who can charm their way through any difficult situation. Moreover, it is unnecessary that the leader possess the expertise and develop the solution; rather, the leader must possess the ability to organize, lead, and manipulate team members to work as a group and develop solutions to their problems.

- Type 3 (Reward power): This style is most popular among employees because leaders have the ability to mediate rewards for workers. In fact, senior leaders' strategies are to motivate workers to achieve objectives by giving them rewards. These leaders tend to motivate employees by showing them carrots at the end of a stick. This in turn leads team members to go in the directions the leader desires.

- Type 4 (Legitimate power): In using this very powerful style, leaders have legitimate power. These leaders have the right to exercise influence over their workers. "Legitimate power resides in the position, not the person. Supervisors, judges, police offers, instructors, and parents have the right to control our behavior within certain limits" (Johnson, 2005, p. 10). Such a leader worked quite hard to achieve a high position in the organization or its respective context.

- The Type 5 (Coercive power): Leaders who like to exercise their authority by punishing workers to achieve the organization's goal are using coercive power (Shafritz & Russell, 2005).

Decision Making and Leadership Styles

Decision making is one of the most significant aspects of every leader's job. The leadership styles leaders choose enable them to make decisions to address the problems they encounter in their organizations. When faced with important organizational decisions, leaders demonstrate four decision-making leadership styles, labeled A through D (Howard, 2005).

Leader A (fact based): Leaders who use fact-based techniques can explain what they expect from workers and show priorities for them to follow. Such leaders believe in using data and research to find facts to solve an organization's problems. The fact-based leader does not hesitate to criticize employees who do not work to their full capacity. Leaders who prefer to use a fact-based style also believe in setting tasks for workers (Howard, 2005). They measure all work activities by standards and divide them into different categories. They set timetables for when the work should be completed. They analyze the organization's problems, think critically, and react slowly when implementing solutions. Above all, fact-based leaders believe that the main priority is accuracy.

The Type B (creativity based) leader is based on one's uses creativity and problem-solving skills. This kind of leader "prefers problem-solving techniques that involve artistic, flexible, imaginative, spontaneous, and holistic responses" (Howard, 2005, p. 99). The creativity-based leader's strength is "open communication with workers or followers" (Howard, 2005, p. 99). These leaders believe in asking questions when they encounter problems in their organizations. They are very comfortable discussing organizational problems with workers. They do not hesitate to ask for ideas from lower level workers about how to address a particular problem. Thus, creativity-based leaders are more flexible in decision making.

As an example, Howard (2005) suggested that a creativity-based leadership style can be used to transform ineffective public school districts to efficient ones. The board of trustees should be able to recruit leaders who are flexible and analytical in decision making to address the complex No Child Left Behind law. "The law requires the standard-based curriculum for formal state achievement tests, and school ratings based upon student performance and overall assessments each school" (Howard, 2005, p. 100). The No Child Left Behind law requires new educational leadership that meets changes the law demanded. The creativity-based leadership style can be useful for the No Child Left Behind law because of the flexibility and ability to resolve current problems. Howard supported the notion that this type of leadership style can be used to transform ineffective school districts to efficient ones.

Type C (feelings-based) leaders do not believe in research. They make decisions based on their feelings about people, the task at hand, and the environment. Leaders who prefer to use the feelings-based leadership style ignore facts that are contrary to their ideas. In addition, these leaders do not use data that are incompatible with their views. "They do not use the principals of science to analyze and solve problems" (Howard, 2005, p. 98).

Type D (control/power-based) leaders use a dictatorial style because they prefer to use power to control workers. They expect workers to be submissive to their demands. Control/power-based leaders are not very creative. In addition, they are not flexible in their managerial approaches. They are not the kind of leaders who have the vision to make remarkable changes to transform their organizations. The control/power-based leadership style is merely based on power and control. The heart of this leadership style is authoritarian (Howard, 2005).

Leadership and Surveys

Much research and many surveys have added to the understanding of the characteristics of different leadership styles. Kouzes and Posner (1997) demonstrated that a survey of 800 senior executives in a federal government rated integrity, competence, and leadership as the three characteristics that make up effective public-organization leaders. The Santa Clara University 2-year study of 2,600 top-level corporate managers revealed that the majority agreed that honest, competent, forward-looking, and inspirational are the most important characteristics of leaders. Another study conducted by AT&T of leadership characteristics produced similar results. The best leadership qualities chosen by AT&T managers were honest, responsible, inspiring, courageous, and forward-looking (Kouzes & Posner, 1997), with the majority of the managers choosing honesty as a superior leader trait. The second ranking was competency, followed by forward-looking. The majority of the U.S. public-organization managers agreed that honesty is an essential part of leadership. Only a few percent of the U.S. public in 1985 believed that most corporate executives were honest (Kouzes & Posner, 1997).

Kouzes and Posner (1997) concluded that honesty is a crucial trait for every leader. A leader without honesty cannot be trusted with any responsibility. No one will follow a dishonest leader. The authors argued that "after all, if we are to follow someone willingly, whether it be into Battle or the Boardroom, we first want to assure ourselves that the person is worthy of our trust" (p. 18). Undoubtedly, most people follow leaders who are ethical and trustworthy. Leaders would not gain the respect they deserve unless they can prove they are honest. In addition, "whatever leaders say about their integrity, followers wait to be shown" (Kouzes & Posner, 1997, p. 18).

Followers look at what leaders do to determine whether they are honest. Kouzes and Posner (1997, p. 18) supported the notion that "agreement not followed through, false promises, deceptions, and cover-ups are all examples of indicators that a leader is not honest." They argued that a chief executive who keeps promises is an honest leader.

Competence is another essential quality of good leaders. Kouzes and Posner (1997) reinforced the notion that leaders must be able to prove they are competent. More importantly, they must be able to explain their ideas and show they know how to do the job. Kouzes and Posner demonstrated this idea:

> The higher the rank of the leader, the more people demand to see demonstrated abilities in strategic planning and policymaking. If a company desperately needs to clarify its distinctive ills and marker positions, a CEO with savvy in competitive marketing may be perceive as a fine leader. (p. 19)

Leadership and Organization Performance

Public managers can demonstrate their competency by improving organizational performance. Additionally, they should provide the right strategies to mobilize the workforce to achieve the mandated purpose. The new public-organization leaders' competency must be judged on how they look at performance standards. Behn (2004) illustrated that the private sector devotes significant resources in developing incentive plans to improve managerial capacity and organizational performance" (p. 6). New public-management leaders must prove they are capable of finding ways to diminish bureaucracy to improve performance.

Another important reason public-management performance is quite weak is that no standard incentive plan exists to improve managerial capacity, and public organizations spend fewer resources than private-sector firms in developing effective incentive standards to improve organizational performance. Most private organizations have better incentive and performance standards than governmental agencies. Behn (2004) illustrated that the private sector devotes significant resources to developing incentive plans to improve managerial capacity and organizational performance. Behn contended that public-organization leaders spend a long time jumping between multiple tasks without seeking ways to improve the organization's performance. They spend considerable time updating mission statements without focusing on accomplishing the organization's objective.

Performance Evaluation and Data

More importantly, public-organization leaders should use performance evaluation and data to monitor their plans and programs. Behn (2004) reinforced the notion that new public-management leaders must monitor performance data so they know whether the organization is heading in the right direction. The data helped track workers' performance and checked whether they followed organizational objectives. In successful reform public management, leaders must set performance targets. Using these targets, leaders can mobilize the workforce to achieve the organizational goal within the target period. Behn supported the notion that by having the performance target in place, along with precise measurements for evaluation, leaders can motivate workers to work intelligently and energetically to accomplish goals.

It is advisable that leaders have performance evaluations in place. Regular performance evaluations help leaders identify what the organization is lacking, which will enable them to design a plan to rectify the problems that are affecting productivity (Behn, 2004). In addition, evaluations allow leaders to set achievable performance targets. Indeed, public management will transform if leaders can identify workforce performance deficits. Behn emphasized that public organizations have multiple performance deficits, and they are very difficult to identify. It is essential that the reform of public management include identification of the organization's performance deficit.

Performance deficits occur when an organization is not operating at its full potential or capacity. It may be that the organization is unable to meet its intended target due to employees' skill deficiencies or organizational mismanagement. Thus, new public-organization leaders should be measured based on how they identify the workforce's performance deficits. According to Behn (2004), "the requirement of leadership, if individuals at the top of an organizational hierarchy fail to select the performance deficits on which their organization should focus, they have no claim to the title of leader" (p. 11). As suggested by Behn (20004) leaders can measure workers' performance by tracking and comparing monthly activities. Below is an example of a city agency workers' performance data:

Chart 1

Agency Staff Performance Data

Staff Performing at Excellent Threshold.		**Staff Performing at Very Good Threshold.**		
01-2	100%		02-2	89%
01-4	100%		03-5	89%
01-5	100%		05-5	89%
02-3	100%		32-2	89%
03-1	100%		33-1	89%
04-3	100%		11-3	88%
04-4	100%		12-1	88%
04-5	100%		04-2	87%
09-3	100%		12-5	86%
09-4	100%		31-3	86%
11-1	100%		06-3	85%
11-2	100%		12-3	85%
11-5	100%		32-1	85%
31-4	100%		03-3	83%
33-2	100%		05-4	83%
33-5	100%		11-4	83%
Staff Performing at Below Excellent Threshold.		**Staff Performing Below Average Threshold.**		
05-2	97%		05-1	82%
12-4	96%		12-2	81%
01-1	95%		31-1	77%
03-4	95%		32-3	76%
06-1	95%		05-3	71%
06-2	95%			
06-5	95%			
31-5	95%			
32-5	95%			
33-4	95%			
01-3	94%			
02-5	94%			
09-1	94%			
09-2	94%			

31-2	94%
02-4	93%
04-1	93%
03-2	92%
09-5	92%
32-4	92%
02-1	91%
33-3	91%
06-4	90%

Every worker with a caseload was assigned a number, ranging from 01-2 to 33-5. Workers' performance was measured and analyzed. The analysis was based on how long it took a worker to complete or make an eligibility determination on each case. Workers who scored 90% or 100% on performance data completed cases in 12 to 30 minutes. These workers were considered to be performing at or above the excellent-performance threshold, whereas those with scores of 89% to 81% completed cases between 31 and 50 minutes and were considered to be performing between the low and the excellent performance threshold. Those with scores of 77% to 71% completed cases in times of 51 to 100 minutes; these workers were assessed as performing below the low-performance threshold. Clients made numerous complaints that workers wasted too much time between interviews. The Agency measured the length of time each worker used to complete each applicant's case. Although the agency used other instruments to measure performance on work activities, they were not included in this study.

Behn (2004) believed that without knowing the exact workers' performance deficits, leaders cannot prescribe solutions to transform public management. If leaders identify performance deficits, they can introduce new polices or strategies to close the deficits. It is very important that the leader publish performance data so all workers know their status. With the publishing of performance data, employees are able to know whether they are heading in the right direction. Additionally, they are able to recognize their weaknesses and find out how to improve their performance. "The leaders of the organization need to verify that people are pursuing their targets.... They need to check for a variety of distortions in which achieving the target may not have contributed significantly to accomplishing the mission" (p. 19). Above all, the gradual transformation of public bureaucracy will materialize if leaders set performance targets for every employee and department.

Effective leaders produce good results through performance management. Performance management can be an effective way to change public bureaucracy through the restructuring of the managerial system. Indeed, public-management leaders will gain a better result by designing a management system that focuses on achieving organizational goals. "Performance management is what leaders do; it is the systematic integration of an organization's efforts to achieve its objectives (Shafritz & Russell, 2005, p. 313).

Indeed, the strategy of the performance-management system enables public leaders to know each standard that has been set in place, which is followed to achieve goals. It gives a clear picture of each stage and what needs to improve the organization's performance and to achieve the intended purpose. An example of performance management evaluation is illustrated in Chart 2:

Napoleon Imarhiagbe, Ph.D.

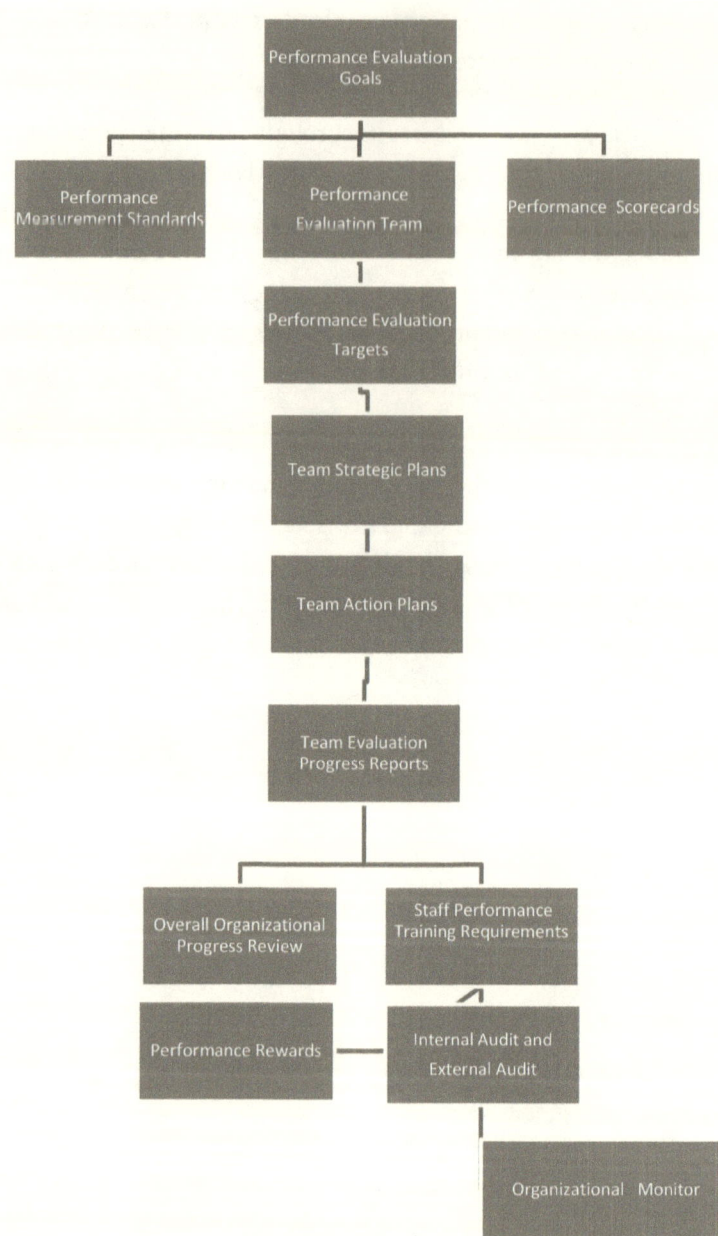

Chart 2

Organization Performance and Employees' Ideas

Having performance data and evaluations in place is very important. However, there are other things leaders can take to improve production such as using employees' ideas to improve work activities. Smith (1997) illustrated that in the past 30 years, Japanese business leaders have made a much greater transformation than U.S. business leaders by improving performance through employees' ideas. The reason for this success was that the Japanese companies used employees' ideas more than the U.S. companies. "In the typical 1,000-person Japanese company, 778 people submit 25,328 new ideas and suggestions. In a typical American company of the same size in which only 90 people submit ideas in which fewer than 35 are implemented" (Smith, 1997, p. 189).

Where employee suggestions are used, an organization totally transforms because employees are excited to see that their ideas have been use to resolve the organization's problems. In fact, when employees' suggestions are implemented, it helps boost their energy; consequently, it improves their performance significantly. The transformation of public organizations can take place easily if leaders consider employees' ideas. New public-management leaders can use employees' ideas to cut down waste in public bureaucracy. Employees' ideas help identify problems, reduce errors, and improve performance. Smith illustrated how some companies used employees' suggestions to improve their performances.

- Harley-Davison saved $3,000 in one 30-day program.
- Holly Farms identified $1,000,000 in savings during a 4-week program.
- Eaton Corporation gained 944 ideas from a workforce of 113 people, reaching 100 percent participation.
- Parker Hannifin Corporation submitted 409 ideas from 103 employees.
- National Semiconductor saved $3,600,000 using idea campaigns,
- The U.S. Park Service made over 12, 000 suggestions with an approval rate of 75% (Smith, 1997, p. 200)

Training and Performance

The improvement of public employees' performance through training is very important; However, leaders also require training. Public organizations need well-trained leaders who have the capability to bring out the best performance in workers. By offering leadership training to public-organization leaders, organizations will experience improved performance. Followers will also experience improved performance. Indeed, the teaching of leadership can be one important contribution to effective leadership performance. A well-trained leader is capable of buoying any organization from zero production to 100%. Leadership training will help restructure bureaucracy. Koestenbaum (1991) asserted that public-management leaders should teach how to challenge, provoke, and motivate workers to be more productive. These leaders should be taught how to address multiple tasks, especially bureaucracy. Leadership training will enable public-organization leaders to be better prepared to handle the uncertainty in public management. Leadership, whether in a public or private sector, should teach everyone because all are capable of being a leader. Koestenbaum contended that most people do not believe leaders can learn and that only a few people understand leadership; as a result, few people choose to be leaders. Koestenbaum emphasized that no one should think leaders are born: "Leadership ability, skill, and even charisma can be acquired and, if already present, can be improved and put to more effective use" (p. 66). Koestenbaum created a formula as one way to approach leadership training is by using Empower (E), Autonomy (A), Direction (D), and Support(S). The formula is $E=AxDxS$:

- E—Leaders *empower* employees to be creative.
- A—Leaders *challenge* workers to work autonomously.
- D—Leaders show workers the *direction.*
- S—Leaders give workers the necessary *support.*

Koestenbaum (1991) demonstrated that "we multiply the leadership virtues with each other to show that a zero in one area gives you a product of zero" (p. 51). For the workforce to be effective, the four categories should be operating in full capacity. Leaving any of the elements behind will invalidate the entire process.

Public organization policies are complex and change rapidly. As a result, public-organization leaders must not only use their managerial skills to manage their organizations, but also transformational model as a way to respond to increasingly complex situations. Ault and Brown's (1997) article, "Correctional Excellence: Leadership Development" illustrates how public-manager leaders rethink their strategies to manage organizational change. The authors emphasized that leadership is necessary to provide vision and direction to rectify the problems of the rapidly growing prison population in the United States where the population of correctional organizations has increased dramatically in past decades. Statistically, 3% of the U.S. population is in jail or some kind of correctional facility. "Close to one-million men and women are in federal or state prisons, more than half a million are in local jails, almost three- quarters of a million are on parole and three million are on probation" (Ault & Brown, 1997 p.134). They used a comparative model to support the position that correctional organizations need leaders who would provide ideas for an alternative prison, which would lessen the prison population. They argued that leadership in correctional organizations should have the capacity to maintain a transformative approach.

Leaders must have the will, the power, and ideas that match changes in today's public organizations (Ault & Brown, 1997). Indeed, new leaders must be able to learn and introduce new ideas to address the rapidly changing workforce and environment. Barbuto and Burbach (2006) supported the notion that leadership's ability to manage complex management problems is quite essential. The ideas of leadership have changed tremendously compared to past decades. The modern leader's focus is on the transformative approach. Barbuto and Burbach asserted that transformational leaders can change public organizations by providing the ideas and strategies for workers to follow. Importantly, transformational leaders are capable of enhancing workers' skills through their visions and ideas. "Transformational leaders are actively engaged within their organization and feel empowered; because they believe that they can influence their environment" (Barbuto & Burbach, 2006, p. 54).

New public-organization leaders will need development and cultivation. Executive leadership can learn, and sometimes require on-the-job training. Current, traditional-management processes seem to prepare future leaders for repetitive tasks, providing a very narrow environment for organizational change: "Skill acquired in this way often prepare the new executive to be reactive and to repeat his or her experiences.... But normally the future differs from the past, and executives can find themselves ill-prepared for the future" (Ault & Brown, 1997, para 9).

Without a doubt, leaders require training and experience. Public bureaucracy requires to have leaders who are creative and possess the vision to approach any difficult task. They must also have the intellectual capacity to overcome any organizational change. In this century, leaders must have all the skills that will enable them to penetrate the "bureaucratic missiles" or the calamity that comes with public management. They must be able to provide ideas to handle any changes, whether in a public bureaucracy or private organization, and no matter the difficulty (Haff, 2003).

In fact, most of the studies examined in this book were able to present strong arguments that public bureaucracy is ineffective and needs to be improved. However, attention was not paid to the issue that public organizations are unable to provide quality services to clients because of their lack of funds. In addition, public-organization leaders and employees are underpaid compared with their counterparts in private sector. These issues should be explored in future studies, to determine how to improve the service provided by public organizations.

Nevertheless, in this study, various research data were gathered and analyzed. Most data came from primary sources. Most studies examined were research conducted on leadership styles in private and nonprofit organizations. The staff-performance data were analyzed to demonstrate how an agency could measure workers' monthly activities and performance. The data analysis determined how one could improve public organizations' performance.

Recommendations

The transformation of public organizations will be successful if leaders are able to identify workers' performance deficits. Having performance data at hand, leaders are able to know whether the organization is heading in the right direction. With performance data, leaders are able to develop new ideas to revamp the public-management system. Additionally, leaders should analyze monthly performance-data reports to refocus their strategy and achieve their organizations' goals (Behn, 2004).

Moreover, leaders should have good strategic planning skills and be able to demonstrate the kind of reform they want. They must have the ability to define the goals and objectives. Leaders should also have the capability to demonstrate tasks and expectation from workers. In addition, they should make sure workers are involved in problem-solving processes (Howard, 2005). Additionally, organizations should use the following ideas to improve production:

- Increase the salaries for those in leadership positions to attract quality leaders to public organizations (Borjas, 2003).
- Develop a scorecard to evaluate work activities.
- Develop strategies and ideas, set directions and targets, and put more resources into achieving organizational goals.

Noticeably, a leader who has the right ideas, strategies, direction, and target, without enough resources cannot meet his or her goals. In addition, a plan without resources cannot be carried out. Therefore, resources are one of the significant tools for leaders to have in order to accomplish their goals. This recommendation is represent by the following chart. The importance of the radial chart is that it refocuses leaders on achieving organizational objectives. It also enables leaders to know that there is a need to have enough resources in addition to the right ideas, direction and strategies used to meet the target that has been set, which brings the organization closer to achieving goals.

Chart 3

Conclusion

Government organizations must rely on leaders with the potential to reform traditional public bureaucracy. New public-organization leaders must be willing to study the problems inherent in traditional bureaucracy to make effective changes. Indeed, the obligation of new public-organization leaders is to set the direction and standards to address public management's problems. They must have the right strategies and visions that will enable them to reduce the red tape in public bureaucracy. As a result, having these will pave a way for the reform of public management. Public-administration leaders should be able to use employees' suggestions to improve performance. Good leaders are not afraid of failure, and are willing to test different ideas to help their organizations work better. More importantly, they are quite confident and do not hesitate to set timetables for when their plans will be achieved.

The search for quality leaders to reform public organizations is quite necessary because most experts see public bureaucracy as a hindrance to effective service delivery. They believe bureaucracy slows down the work process. Without a doubt, U.S. public administration is not a perfect system, but by using effective leadership skills, public managers are able to resolve some complications that come with public bureaucracy.

Additionally, by introducing good leadership skills, leaders are able to implement new ideas to transform public organizations, which will enable them to manage as effectively as private and nonprofit organizations.

Based on the research findings, effective reform of public bureaucracy will materialize, if leaders use the following strategies:

- Identify workers' performance deficits.
- Use the analysis of performance data to identify workers 'performance deficits.
- Use performance data to introduce new training programs to improve workers' performance as well as that of the organization.
- Offer leadership trainings to all new public-organization leaders.
- Focus the training on how leaders can reform public bureaucracy to become more effective.
- Through leadership training, new public-organization leaders will effectively address multiple tasks and complex public management.
- Through leadership training, leaders are able to gain more knowledge on how to restructure public bureaucracy. Consequently, bureaucracy will no longer present a dilemma; it will become a better system to deliver public services than previously.

The effective reform of public bureaucracy will serve as a new managerial approach to public management. Leaders will improve public organizations' performance in this early 21st century using fact-based leadership styles as a guideline. One reason is that fact-based leadership is effective in addressing public organizations' multiple tasks. According to Howard (2005), "Fact based leaders are comfortable with people, tasks, and environments that requires facts, logic ,theories, scientific applications, analysis, quantitative, mathematical, and technical processes. They establish high standards of quantitative behavior and expectations from employees and themselves" (p. 99). One definition of fact-based leadership style is the ability of leaders to seek perfection in themselves and others (Howard, 2005). Leaders who use the fact-based leadership style are very careful when taking actions to address complex issues. In fact, they are quite meticulous and do not "rush to judgment," because public policies are delicate and change rapidly (Howard, 2005). Moreover, the fact-based leadership style enables public-organization leaders to use data analysis to improve work activities and strengthen the workforce. In addition, it enables them to set standards for workers to follow. In fact, it brings out the best in workers and significantly energizes them to contribute more to the success of the organization (Howard, 2005). More importantly, it enables managers to reduce errors made by workers. In fact, leaders can learn how to use a fact-based leadership style to reduce bureaucracy in public organizations, which has hindered the effective delivery of public services.

References

Ault, A. L., & Brown, R. M., Jr. (1997). Correctional excellence: Leadership development. *Corrections Today, 59*(2), 134.

Anechiarico, F., & Jacobs, B. J. (1996). *The pursuit of absolute integrity.* Chicago, IL: University of Chicago Press.

Angelucci, P. A. (2005). For leadership effectiveness, look inside nursing. *Management Journal.*

Barbuto, J. E., Jr., & Burbach, M. E. (2006). The emotional intelligence of transformational leaders: A field study of elected officials. *The Journal of Social Psychology, 146,* 51–64. doi:10.3200/SOCP.146.1.51-64.

Behn, R. D. (2004, May). *Performance leadership II better practices that can ratchet up performance.* Cambridge, MA: Harvard University, John F. Kennedy of School of Government.

Borjas, G. J. (2003). *Wage structures and the sorting of workers into the public sector.* Washington, DC: Brookings Institution.

Haff, T. J. (2003, April). *The power of frontline workers in transforming government: The Upstate New York Veterans Health Care Network.* Albany: State University of New York School of Public Health.

Howard W. C. (2005). Leadership: Four styles. *Education, 126,* 384–391.

Johnson E. C. (2005). *Meeting the ethical challenge of leadership: Casting light or shadow* (2nd ed.). Thousand Oaks, CA: Sage.

Kobrak, P. (2002). *The political environment of public management.* New York, NY: Longman.

Koestenbaum, P. (1991). *Leadership: The inner side of greatness.* San Francisco, CA: Jossey-Bass.

Kouzes, M., & Posner B. Z. (1997). *The leadership challenge: How to get extraordinary things done in organizations.* San Francisco, CA: Jossey-Bass.

Maccoby M. (1983). *The leader: A new face American management.* New York, NY: Simon and Schuster.

Milakovich, M. E., & Gordon, G. J. (2001). *Public administration in America* (7th ed.). Boston MA: St. Martin's.

Shafritz, J. M., & Russell, E. W. (2005). *Introducing public administration* (4th ed.). New York, NY: Pearson Education.

Smith, P. (1997). *The new leader: Bringing creativity and innovation to the workplace.* Delray Beach, FL: St. Lucie Press.

Stillman, R., II. (1996). *The American bureaucracy: The core of modern government.* Chicago, IL: Nelson-Hall.

Syett, D. (1992). *Frontiers and leadership: An essential reader.* Cambridge, MA: Blackwell.

CHAPTER 2

DEPTH COMPONENT

Introduction

The depth component examines how leaders respond and manage organizational change. One primary goal of a leader is to find a way to introduce new ideas and implement changes. Most importantly, leadership is crucial when an organization is undergoing changes. Organizational change is meant to achieve resourceful development in the future. How do leaders implement changes to obtain a productive workforce and increase efficiency? Specifically, organizational change is about setting the tone for new directions. Organizational change is about a leader asking the right questions: Are we doing the right thing? Are we on the right track? Are we following the mission statement? Are we complying with government' policies? What can we do to reduce our errors and improve performance? A leader must ask but also answer these questions, while trying to improve efficiency and develop a more productive workforce.

Change in the public sector is also about organization leaders changing procedures to comply with new government's regulations, which, for example, authorize an increase in public assistance to citizens, or building more shelters for people who are homeless. Organizational change is a test of a leader's ability to execute change because employees and humans by nature are likely to resist change. Thus, organizational change rarely occurs voluntarily. Leaders are forced to change their procedures and policies.

Changes in public management, however, are different from changes in the private sector because governmental policies govern public organizations. Importantly, leaders who run public organizations face far greater problems than leaders of private and nonprofit organizations. One major reason for this is that public-organization leaders must implement laws passed by legislatures, the judiciary, and chief executives. In addition, they are not only responsible for the welfare of their workers, but also for the general public. Additionally, leaders are expected to handle multiple tasks that may be beyond their control. Therefore, this chapter explores the qualities that leaders need in responding and managing changes in public management. However, this does not means that a leader in a public organization ignores change or is free from change. On the contrary, this fact requires leaders to use their leadership and managerial skills even more efficiently, because the stakeholders involved in the process, that is, those who are going to be affected by the leader's and teams' performance, are governmental and legislative bodies. Failure to comply with their needs or deliver their desired outcomes would lead not only to bankruptcy, but also to serious legal issues.

Organizational Change in Different Sectors

The decision to make change in private sectors belongs to the leaders or CEOs of a company or a corporation. Public administrators cannot make change without the authorization of lawmakers. More importantly, public-organization leaders are measured in terms of how they manage changes authorized by lawmakers, and how the leader's actions affect the delivery of public services, unlike business managers who, are measured based on the amount of corporate profit (Mises, 1962). Indeed, the success or failure of organizational change depends on how the changes that are implemented generate profits for private organizations. Mises (1962) contended that "in public administration there is no market for achievements; this makes it indispensable to operate public office according to principles entirely different from those applied under the profit motive" (p. 47).

Another problem is that public organizations are complex and change rapidly. Public bureaucracy is too complicated for leaders to master change (Shafritz & Russell, 2005). Public bureaucracies are used to one standard and procedure, which is often very difficult to change. Moreover, bureaucracies are very difficult to change because of the structure and ways workers are trained to operate. "Actions based upon training and skills which have been successfully applied in the past result in inappropriate responses under changed conditions" (Shafritz & Russell, 2005, p. 266).

Also, public bureaucracies are very difficult for leaders to manage because they believe bureaucracies are seeded with incompetence. In addition, public bureaucracies are very slow to respond to change. Shafritz and Russell (2005) demonstrated,

> One of the perennial complaints about bureaucracy is its lack of responsiveness to changing conditions. However, this notorious slowness to change is very often a function of its legal mandate.... This alleged slowness, from another point of view, is simply its obedience to the laws. (p. 265)

Bryant (1998) also supported the notion that public bureaucracies progress slowly: "Public service bureaucracies, particularly large ones, indicate they are frequently too slow and cumbersome, inefficient and ineffective, unresponsive and unaccountable, and unable to deal with fast-paced change creatively" (Bryant, 1998, p. 102). One reason for the slowness of the bureaucratic process is that leaders spend too much time planning for the implementation of new laws; also, some leaders may be confused about how to interpret those laws. As a result, it is quite difficult for them to develop new strategies to comply with government's policies. Therefore, public-management leaders must be able to understand every aspect of change, and they must be creative to manage change effectively.

Reasons for Organizational Change

Several reasons exist for organizational change. Leaders usually change their organization's direction (both public and private) when government policies or regulations shift (Dean, 2001). Bechard and Harris (1977) illustrated how leaders changed their organizations' policies because of new laws: "The federal government of the United States has required that all organizations doing business with the government have affirmative action programs specific action plans" (p. 17). Affirmative action laws were meant to give special privilege to veterans, minorities, and women in recruitment and selection practices; those who were underrepresented in the workplace. As a result, some organizations developed a program specifically designed to hire more minorities to diversify their workforces, whereas other organizations included affirmative-action programs as a part of the personnel system, addressing issues regarding minorities' employment. All organizations that were affected by federal-government policies were compelled to develop strategies to comply with the new affirmative-action laws.

Private organizations or nonprofit organizations can be forced to change the way they market or sell their products because of new laws passed by Congress or interpreted by a court decision (Dean, 2001). Some organizations may be forced to change the way they do business because they are not meeting government standards. For example, "The Federal Communication Commission (FCC) laws forced AT& T to form a fully separate utility (first American Bell, then AT& T information systems); trust laws created an even playing field for domestic competition" (Dean, 2001, p. 20).

Leaders are obliged to make changes that will enable them to comply with the way the government interprets how businesses should operate. Public as well as private leaders, therefore, must be well prepared to respond to government laws and manage them effectively. One more aspect that causes organizations—private or government—to implement or adopt change is stagnancy. Consider the example of stagnant water as it becomes host to certain insects and algae production. However, the continuously flowing, course changing river water always stays fresh and is potable. Hence, any company that wants to continue its success needs to continuously bring changes to its organization. Whether change manifests in the structure of the organization, policies, or implementation plans, it has always proven to be fruitful to do so. More importantly, leaders must make sure the organizational goals and changes in government policies are effectively carried out.

Managing Organizational Change

Managing organizational change is a difficult undertaking; this is why it has provoked extensive research in an effort to provide guidelines for leaders to address bureaucratic change. Companies that decided they would not maintain their strategies throughout their era in the business market assigned dedicated and strong leaders to lead the change. Organizations want their change process to succeed such that they even create a change-implementation plan; however, even after investing so much in this process, they may fail to invest in the process that comes after implementation: the change-management phase. This phase is the most vital phase because not only does it ensure proper implementation of the entire change, but also highlights the discrepancies in the process; by highlighting such mistakes, leaders can amend their change-management and implementation plans. For instance, Bechard and Harris (1977) demonstrated the methods public and other leaders can use to respond to and manage change:

- Diagnosing the present condition, including the need for change
- Setting goals and defining the state or condition after the change
- Defining the transition states between the present and the future
- Developing strategies and action plans for managing this transition;
- Evaluating the change effort; and stabilizing the new condition and establishing a balance between stability and flexibility. (p. 17)

Leaders must have the capability to implement change and be able to ensure that changes made are sustained in the organization. They must be able to reinforce change whether it is set by them or by the government. Leaders must first accept that without changes, the way the organization performs may never improve (Gomolski, 2000). In addition, leaders must accept that change involves a process; one that may not be a smooth journey.

Change is sometimes a painful experience, but it is necessary to improve an unproductive workforce (Daiziel & Schoonover, 1988). Effective leaders are able to implement or adapt to any change no matter the difficulty. A leader must have the vision and ideas to motivate workers to accept new polices that will eventually change the old ways. Moreover, leaders should be able to convince workers that changes are better for them as well as the organization (Daiziel & Schoonover, 1988).

Daiziel and Schoonover (1988) reinforced this notion "by offering straightforward practices and frameworks for change, change leaders can provide productive directions for other to follow while calming concerns" (p. 7). In fact, organizational change enables leaders to cut down waste and improve worker productivity. It also gives leaders the opportunity to implement their visions for the future and for the advancement of the organization. In addition, change enables leaders to see what they are doing wrong and develop ideas to rectify problems. Organizational change is about management renovation and improvement of the organization's performance.

Steers (1991) demonstrated some effective ways leaders can respond to organizational change:

- Recognizing and encouraging subordinate needs for outcomes that leaders can control;
- Increasing personal payoffs to subordinates for effective performance or goal attainment;
- Clarifying the path to those payoffs, through either coaching or additional direction;
- Helping subordinates clarify expectancies;
- Reducing obstacles or frustrations that inhibit goal attainment; and
- Increasing opportunities for personal satisfaction from effective performance (p. 386)

Additionally, leaders can facilitate organizational change by providing resources to workers and getting them involved in the process. Moreover, effective leaders should be able to clarify any misunderstanding among workers about the organizational change or the change process. Conflicts among workers must be resolved by leaders. Indeed, leaders must be able to maintain or provide stability during the organizational-change process. Steers (1991) affirmed that leaders are likely to accomplish their aim in the organizational change if they are able to "provide specific guidance, standards, and schedules of work, as well as rules and regulations; lets subordinates know what is expected of them" (p. 387). A leader might also want to encourage as well as consider worker's suggestions about how to implement organizational change. Employee suggestions are very valuable because their jobs are directly affected by the organizational change. In fact, workers' cooperation is very important for leaders in setting new directions for the organization. This is because employees and leaders are in the situation. Moreover, some employees have a wealth of experiences and ideas that are vital to the implementation of the change leaders may need.

In any organization, governmental or private, leaders should involve employees in the organizational-change process. This is very important because the majority of jobs are performed by employees. For leaders to have an effective change and ultimate success, they must set standards and challenge workers to perform very well in their tasks. Steers (1991) reinforced this notion: Good "leaders set challenging goals, emphasize improvement in performance, and establish high expectations of subordinates' ability to meet improved standards of excellence" (p. 387). These recommendations are vital for leaders, especially those who want to make effective and efficient changes to the organization. Organizational change is not an easy task. However, leaders who plan and prepare for change are capable of achieving their goals. Sometimes, leaders may have to take drastic action, replacing workers or subordinates who are resistant to change (Wilson, 1989). Wilson offered an example of actions that a leader look to reinforce change in a public organization:

Caspar Weinberger did this at the Federal Trade Commission where, in order to instill a new sense of vigor and commitment to consumer protection, he replaced eighteen of the thirty-one top staff members and about two hundred of the nearly six hundred staff attorneys. Weinberger and his successors as FTC chairman brought in new people specially recruited because they supported a new way of defining the agency's core task. (1989, p. 231)

Additionally, leaders can create special units and train workers to perform tasks to implement the organization's new policies. Training will enable the organization to achieve changes that are required. Leaders can also persuade workers to support the organization's new initiatives by promising rewards. Wilson (1989) reinforced this notion: "the executive who wishes to make changes has to create incentives for subordinates to think about" (p. 231). Such rewards help leaders energize workers to contribute more to the success of changes leaders want to make. Rewards may also convince workers and subordinates that the new change brings benefits to them.

Leadership and Resistance to Change

Change is very difficult to reinforce in public organizations because of the public bureaucratic system of management. Employees want to maintain the same standards and procedures because they are stuck in a bureaucratic-management system. In fact, there is always potential resistance to change in public organizations, especially if employees are asked to undertake a new task (Milakovich & Gordon, 2001). One reason is that public employees' unions make it very difficult for leaders to implement new polices. If change is going to cause substantial profits and would result in a company's development, why would anyone resist change? The answer to this question might simply be that they do not like their leader; the leader might not possess a charming personality. The leader might not be an expert leader or even a good leader, who might not be listening to the teams or must be causing more damage than the change would bring in profit. To avoid these pitfalls, a leader must always listen to employees and not only involve them in the change-management process, but also make them stakeholders in this process and key elements of the change the leader is trying to achieve.

Employee unions protect workers from doing extra work (Lipsky, 1980). As a result, leaders are unable to comply with new government policies to change how organizations operate. In addition, civil-service laws are an obstacle for leaders in most public organizations seeking to reinforce change. Workers are also resistant to change if they are not satisfied with the new contract the union negotiated with the mayor or the city council.

Workers may refuse to perform certain tasks that slow down the work process (Lipsky, 1980). For example, police officers can refuse to make arrests if they do not like the new change. Traffic officers can also refuse to reinforce parking regulations to embarrass leaders who called for increases to achieve the organization's new changes. The most common resistance to change in public organizations involves workers going on strike. For example, the New York City transit workers went on strike in December 2005 because the union and the Metropolitan Transit Authority (MTA) failed to reach a new contract agreement; remaining issues were employees' pensions and medical-insurance benefits.

In addition, public employees may decline to comply with the new change if they are not promised rewards. Indeed, leaders depend on subordinates to execute new polices; without subordinates or lower level workers, the new policy may never be implemented. Lipsky (1980) reinforce this idea: "as judges who informally allocate sentencing decisions to probation officers are dependent on their hierarchical subordinates for the smooth functioning of their jobs" (p. 25). Thus, leaders must ensure their subordinates are satisfied, even if that involves several compromises with a union.

One reason a welfare agency's employees resist organizational change is the increase in caseloads or tasks (Lipsky, 1980). Employees should be assured that the new change will not increase their caseloads. Moreover, workers should be promised or assured that new policies will not affect their job security or long-term careers in the organization. Milakovich and Gordon (2001) illustrated one classic example of how public employees are resistance to organizational change:

> Inglewood, California, has used one-man refuse trucks for more than a decade at significantly reduced cost and with fewer injuries and greater satisfaction for personnel. Informed of the one-man trucks, the sanitation director in an eastern city using four men to a truck said he did not believe it. Having confirmed that they

were in use, he opined that Inglewood's street and contours were different from his cities. Convinced that conditions in both places were generally the same, he lamented that his constituents would never accept the lower level of service. Persuaded that the levels of service were equal, he explained that the sanitation men would not accept a faster pace and harder work conditions. Told that the Inglewood sanitation men prefer the system because they set their own pace and suffer fewer injuries caused by careless coworkers, the director prophesied that the city council would never agree to such a large cutback in manpower. Informed of Inglewood's career development plan to move sanitation men into other city departments, the director pointed out he was responsible only for sanitation. (p. 404)

For organizational change to be effective and actualized, leaders as well as workers must support it. Leaders must be genuinely interested in the change process. In addition, leaders must be dedicated to achieving the change proposed by policymakers or the city council. Most importantly, lawmakers must provide leaders with enough resources to implement the new changes. Lipsky (1980) asserted, "most executives profess that their organizations do not have sufficient resources or at least are hampered by resource constraint" (p. 33). Without enough resources, leaders may not be able to make a smooth transition to achieve the change required by the organization. Policymakers pass new laws to improve public organizations' performance, but enough funds are not usually provided for the leaders of the agencies to implement these new policies.

In addition, laws passed by Congress for increased free medical insurance to the poor and minorities may suffer from lack of funding. Consequently, the number of people seeking free medical care increases because the new law authorizes free benefits: "It has often been observed that utilization increases when public services are expanded. Hospital emergency rooms become inundated because they provide free medical care" (Lipsky, 1980, p. 33). For leaders of the agency to meet public demand, they need more resources to hire workers to provide benefits for those who are eligible for the program. Lipsky (1980) affirmed that a social worker's caseload will increase significantly if agency leaders are unable to secure adequate resources to hire more workers to perform the job. This is usually the case in public organizations where leaders face several difficulties in implementing new policies required by lawmakers.

Another important reason organizational change is very difficult to reinforce is that workers are afraid that the change may affect their self-interest. They are afraid that organizational change leads to job consolidation or downsizing. Kirkpatrick (1985) supported the notion that employees are resistant to change because they worry their positions may be eliminated through the new changes. Additionally, employees are concerned their salaries or bonuses may be reduced. Sometimes, overtime hours are decreased or abolished. Moreover, employees fear the new procedures and policies will change their tasks and job classifications. Robbins (1987) affirmed that organizational change may threaten employee self-interest because they have invested more in specific skills. Workers are afraid their skills will become irrelevant and their leaders may force them to undergo another training to uplift their skills to meet the quality the new change demands.

Kirkpatrick (1985, p. 8) reinforces the notion that workers fear new policies and ideas because their "job title, responsibility, or authority might be reduced from an important one to a lesser one with loss of status and recognition from other." Most employees also wonder if managers will ask them to perform additional tasks. Kirkpatrick asserted that any organizational change requires more effort from workers, and most of them are not happy about it: "Whenever change requires more time and effort, people are apt to resent and even resist them, particularly if no rewards accompany the extra effort" (1985, p. 88).

Employees oftentimes do not fully understand the reason for change (Robbins, 1987). Sometimes leaders fail to elucidate to their workers why the organization needs a new direction. As a result, employees feel "left in the dark" and confused about what is going to happen if the new change is implemented (Dean, 2001). Bad decisions and inadequate execution of changes by leaders lead to commotion and resentment among workers (Dean, 2001). What is more important is that a lack of understanding among workers makes it impossible for leaders to draw support to the new polices and change the organizational procedures or work processes.

Organizational change cannot be possible without leaders developing strategies to remove any resistance to the policy change. Additionally, leaders must be able to withstand criticism about changes they have made. Gomolski (2000) explicated that "leaders must have the power to reinforce change effects at all levels and the stamina and tenacity to withstand widespread criticism and resistance" (p. 98). Despite an effort by employees to maintain the status quo, it is the duty of the leader to reinforce the policy that will enable them to achieve needed changes. According to Daiziel and Schoonover (1988), leaders must have the capability to control the potential chaos and obstacles that come with organizational change.

Overcoming Resistance to Change and Leadership

One way to overcome resistance to change is by designing a system to motivate workers to embrace the new change. Adding to what has been stated earlier, a plan should be in place before implementing the new change to give incentives to workers, such as bonuses, traveling allowances, extra minutes for lunch, more vacation days, a gym room, and if necessary, increased salaries. These rewards will enable workers to know that the new change is beneficial to them. As a result, these rewards it will incite them to work energetically to support the changes initiated by their leaders (Johnson, 2005). Undoubtedly, changes in an organization are leaders' responsibility. Therefore, they must be able to execute strategies to overcome hindrances to an effective change or outcome. Changing an organization's procedures and polices is a difficult task, but better planning enables leaders to achieve the results they want. First, to manage change effectively, leaders in public organizations must understand the need for change. They must see change as an opportunity to improve performance. A public organization's leaders should view change as an opportunity to better serve the public (Bryant, 1998).

Additionally, leaders must see change as a way to reduce waste and bureaucracy in public management. Importantly, leaders must accomplish goals by inspiring workers to perform tasks better than their expectations. Leaders should invest more resources in the areas that would lead to meaningful change. Daiziel and Schoonover (1988) affirmed that "leaders avoid wasted resources, false starts, and failed initiatives and they quickly capitalize on investments in time and resources by making the change processes work" (p. 26). More importantly, leaders should be able to motivate workers to achieve a common goal. They must make sure that everyone is on "the same page" (Daiziel & Schoonover, 1988).

Dean (2001) contended that workers need to be reminded of why the organization needs to change its direction. In addition, all employees need to understand the importance of the organization's new directions and what is required from them to make the change materialize. To fully implement change, leaders must try to understand the reasons workers resist change. Steers (1991, p. 62) said "the success or failure of change efforts rests not only on accurate identification of the problem and successful reduction of resistance to change but also on the appropriateness of the selected strategy for implementing the change." In addition, leaders must be flexible and innovative to be effective in implementing change (Robbins, 1987). Leaders must also have ideas and visions to make change happen. During the organizational transition, it is advisable that leaders ask questions: "What is our core purpose? What do we stand for? What is our vision for serving the new market place needs?" (Dean, 2001, p. 45) This strategic planning enables leaders to refocus employees on achieving the proposed change.

Dean (2001) claimed that poor planning and lack of communication by leaders slows the change process, which may lead to fruitless results or the inability to achieve the intended purpose. Leaders are able to make an adequate transformation when they have the right plan in place. Leaders must have a clear objective and involve employees in the implementation of the new policy to make the change happen. This will ensure that the organization succeeds in the new state, and achieves its goals (Dean, 2001).

Leadership Models for Managing Change

Four kinds of leadership models are useful for leaders to manage change: transformational, transactional, developmental, and transitional. The transformational model can be described as a leader's ability to create a new vision and ideas to achieve what might not have been possible. Indeed, the transformational model enables leaders to transform their organizations to become successful through their visions and creativity. "A person who could totally transform an embedded organizational culture by creating a new vision of and for the organizational, and successfully selling that vision-by rallying commitment and loyalty to make the vision become reality is a transformational leader" (Shafritz & Russell, 2005, p. 374). The transformational model means the leader is able to fully engage and connect with workers through their visions. For example, "General George S. Patton Jr., who during World War II took charge of a defeated and demoralized American Army in North Africa and transformed it into a winning team" by creating a new vision and ideas for troops to follow (Shafritz & Russell, 2005, p. 373).

The transformational model also enables leaders to plan correctly and set the vision to handle the uncertainty that comes with organizational change (Dean, 2001). As illustrated by Shafritz and Russell (2005), "transformational leaders are those rare individuals who can lead employees through their fears and uncertainties to the realization of the new vision" and achieve the change that has been proposed by them (p. 373). Indeed, transformational leaders have the faith, vision, and will to succeed in making a transition to change. Moreover, the model gives leaders the vision and ideas to convince employees that change is essential to improve their work activities and bring efficiency to the organization.

The transactional leadership model is about a leader making change by appealing to workers' self-interest, averring that the change will be beneficial to them if they embrace the organization's new policies. Indeed, the transactional-leadership model is about "give and take." The notion is that if workers know that their leaders will increase their salaries, they are likely to support the new policy. Steers (1991) demonstrated,

Transactional leaders motivate employees by appealing to self-interest. That is, transactional leaders treat leadership as an exchange that is a "transaction" relationship between themselves and their employees. In essence, they are saying, I will look after your interests if you will look after mine and the company's. (p. 391)

In other words, "your interest is my interest." In the transactional model, leaders are able to implement change by telling workers that both leaders and employees are in the same proverbial boat. Workers are highly motivated if they understand that the organizational changes will suit their interests. What is more important about the transactional-leadership model is that it promotes good working relations between leaders and workers.

The development model is meant to strengthen or rectify existing activities to improve performance and workers' satisfaction. It also signifies that people are capable of changing their attitude toward new policies if leaders provide them with the resources and training to do better. Indeed, the developmental-change model can be used to help instill new skills and sets in motion higher levels of performance. Dean (2001) supported the argument that "when leaders challenge people to excel and provide them the resources and support to do so, this usually produces the necessary motivation for successful development change" (p. 34). For instance, workers are more motivated to do their jobs when they are trained on how to use new computers to improve their work performance. Dean elucidated that in the developmental model, "workers are motivated by the goal to do 'better than' or do 'more of' what is currently done.... The process of development keeps people vibrant, growing, and stretching through the challenge of attainting new performance levels" (2001, p. 34). Additionally, the developmental model is best initiated when leaders raise the performance level by setting new goals. Leaders are able to execute new policies by using the development model to improve workers' performance. This model is also very effective when it is used by leaders to amend new policies during their organization's change process.

The transitional model is meant to replace existing activities or programs with entirely different work. The main notion of the transitional model is that the leader recognizes that something in the existing operation needs to be changed or replaced with newer processes to achieve the organization's goals (Dean, 2001). The transitional model is not about improving work activities, unlike the developmental model.

A good example of the transitional model is when a leader constructs a new road instead of repairing the old one. The transitional-change model is about leaders dismantling old ways and replacing them with new ones. The transitional model also enables leaders to plan correctly. Indeed, using the transitional model, leaders are able to plan for problems they may encounter during the transitional period. Leaders must have the right plan to change from old ways of operation to new ones. Inadequate planning for the transition will lead to organizational confusion, whereby the leader is unable to make transition from the old to the new.

Recommendations

Overcoming employees' resistance to change requires leaders with superb managerial skills to make the change take place. Organizational change is not an easy process, and leaders who have the right strategy and team support are able to achieve the changes they've initiated. Therefore, for an organization's change to be effective, leaders should use the following strategies, drawn from different models and experiences:

- Workers should be retrained for new policies and tasks to achieve the organization's goals.
- Workers who continue to be resistant to change should be transferred or fired (Wilson, 1989).
- Leaders should develop good incentive plans to motivate or convince employees to support the organization's new changes. Employees who supported the organization's changes should be rewarded with cash bonuses or extra days off from work.
- Leaders should use scorecards to monitor how effective the new changes are.
- Leaders should project or set timetables for when the new change will be accomplished.

- Leaders should evaluate new changes that have been made to determine if the company is on the right track. Leaders should develop strategic plans to correct errors and amend areas that are not meeting the organizational goals or require changes.
- Leaders should make sure all members of the organization, from the bottom to top, are "on the same page." In addition, employees should understand every aspect of the new policies to change the organization's direction.
- Leaders should be able to develop alternate plans in case current plans do not materialize. For example, leaders can change from the transformational to the developmental model of addressing organizational change (Dean, 2001).
- Leaders should develop negotiation skills to bargain with employee unions that may not support the proposed change (Lipsky, 1980).
- Leaders can create a special unit to implement new policies, which would eventually change the organization's procedures and directions.

Conclusion

Organizational change is very difficult for leaders to implement or reinforce for numerous reasons, due to the laws that govern public organizations. Most of the time, public organizations' leaders cannot introduce new policies unless policymakers authorize them. Sometimes, a public organization leader is forced to make changes that are conflict with personal interests or the way the leader wants the company or change to be organized because of public laws or court orders.

Indeed, changing a bureaucratic system is not very easy for leaders, because public-organization employees have been trained to perform their tasks in one way. The hierarchy system has no flexibility. Workers still rely on people at the top to make decisions (Gergen & Kellerman, 2003). The fact is, bureaucracy is outdated and should be changed because, as a system of management, it is no longer effective in this modern world (Mises, 1944).

This change requires leaders with the vision and ideas to cut down the bureaucracy in public management. Public bureaucracy is too slow and complicated, and reduces worker performance and the ability to deliver public services effectively. In fact, public bureaucracy cannot be dismantled or abolished, but leaders who have the right strategy and creativity can make the system work efficiently.

Moreover, organizational change is not an easy task for public-management leaders because policymakers do not always provide sufficient resources to implement polices they have proposed. As a result, the change process is very slow and sometimes fails to achieve the intended purpose. Therefore, leaders must be able to mobilize workers and provide sufficient resources to implement the new change effectively. Moreover, one effective way of achieving organizational change is by training employees about new policies. Training provides workers a better understanding of what is required from them to align with the new policies. Additionally, training creates ways for leaders to change the way the public organization operates. More importantly, leaders must be able to interpret public-policy laws and ensure they are not violating laws or implementing the wrong policies. Thus, it is very important that leaders have training on how to interpret government laws or policies.

Organizational change cannot be possible in public organizations without leaders who have the negotiation skills to bargain with various interest groups. Indeed, leaders must have the ability to bargain with public-employee unions to implement new ideas and have the support of the workers. Indeed, change is very difficult to reinforce in public organizations because of civil-service laws. Also, other governmental regulations and laws exist that leaders must follow.

In addition, new public-management leaders must have the managerial skills to overcome any resistance to organizational change. First, they must understand the reasons employees resist change so that they are able to develop strategies to overcome that resistance. They must also be able to convince employees that change is required to improve the organization's performance as well as their work activities (Paul, 1982). Additionally, leaders must have trust and credibility to convince employees to follow them and change the organization's direction. Hacker and Washington (2003) believed that "only executive leadership has the position and potential to successfully initiate strategic change. It is the role of leadership to uncover the need to change and enroll others in the belief that an authentic need exists"(p. 2). Moreover, leaders must have the will and the strategic plans to implement sustainable change in their organizations.

Various leadership models can be useful for leaders to implement changes in public organizations. One effective model is transformational leadership. This model enables leaders to address any organizational change. In fact, the transformational model enables leaders to gain the support of the workers in order to implement the new change successfully. Importantly, leaders who use the transformational model are capable of addressing multiple tasks in public organizations. The transformational model enables leaders to handle complex public-management issues.

Shafritz and Russell (2005) supported the idea that the transformational-leadership model enables leaders to change workers' perceptions about new policies initiated by them. Pillai and Williams (2004) reinforced the idea that in using the transformational model, leaders are taught to engage employees and motivate them to achieve higher levels of service. They added to the argument that "transformational leaders influence followers to higher levels of commitment and performance... and developing individual group members to reach their highest potential" (p. 145).

Another effective leadership model that is useful for leaders in implementing and reinforcing organizational change is the transactional model, which helps leaders overcome employee resistance to change. The transactional model enables leaders to move from an unproductive workforce to an effective one. Leaders who use the transactional model are able to convince their employees to embrace new policies to change the organization's directions. What is more important about this model is that it promotes good relationships between employees and leaders.

Moreover, the transactional model helps leaders boost employee energy, which enables them, in turn, to contribute more to the success of the new policies. Leaders who have the right plan and use leadership models such as the transformational and transactional methods, are able to overcome employee resistance to change, and can implement new policies whether policymakers or the court initiate them. Undoubtedly, public bureaucracies are difficult to change. However, leaders who use the right leadership models and have commitment can introduce new ideas that are effective enough to reduce waste and mismanagement in public organizations. Consequently, this will make public organizations more effective, and better able to deliver services faster than they could before.

Annotated Bibliography

Pillai, R., & Williams, E. A. (2004). Transformational leadership, self-efficacy, group cohesiveness, commitment, and performance. *Journal of Organizational Change Management, 17,* 144–159. doi:10.1108/09534810410530584

Pillai and Williams (2004) explored how a transformational-leadership model can help leaders inspire workers to make an effective change. The transformational model is a way leaders can successfully instigate a change through their visions and creativity. The authors hypothesized that "transformational leaders enhance followers' self-efficacy, which in turn, results in higher performance and commitment" (p.146). The authors demonstrated that:

> The conceptualization of transformational leaders is consistent with the prevalent literature that transformational leaders influence followers to higher levels of commitment and performance by articulating a vision, fostering the acceptance of group goals and developing individual group members to reach their highest potential. (Pillai & Williams, 2004, p. 145)

The authors used a review of the literature to support the notion that the transformational model helps leaders articulate their vision for the future. Leaders who use the transformational model are able to boost workers' morality, motivate them to overcome stressful conditions, and achieve higher performance during a catastrophe. The military and fire departments are very good at using the transformational model to inspire subordinates to take risks. The success of the New York City fire fighters during the September 11 tragedy was the result of their ability to overcome stressful conditions. With the aid of field research, the authors were able to explore "The importance of leadership interventions to train fire department leaders who are then perceived as role models by the fire fighters and who work to reduce stress in one of the most stressful jobs in America" (Pillai & Williams, 2004, p. 144).

Pillai and Williams (2004) concluded that leaders who use the transformational-leadership model are able to motivate workers to make personal sacrifices and work toward a common goal. Leaders place greater emphasis on working toward commitment to collective interests, which result in workers' higher job performance. The authors' research was merely based on primary data and literature-review articles. Most data support the argument that the transformational model enables leaders to use their vision effectively to convince workers who are resistant to change to support new initiatives. The transformational model is quite different from the use of a basic strategic-planning method to accomplish objectives because it focuses on how leaders articulate their ideas and visions to achieve the change workers may have not previously supported.

Dunoon, D. (2002). Rethinking leadership for the public sector. *Australian Journal of Public Administration*, 61(3), 3–18. doi:10.1111/1467-8500.00280

The author's research supported the notion that the transformational model enables leaders to inspire workers to embrace their visions to achieve the change they need. The hypothesis was that the transformational-leadership model, when used by private or public-sector leaders, can change the minds of employees to support their policies use. The heart of this model is that it enables leaders to build momentum for change. The author concluded that leaders are able to overcome resistance to change by using the transformational model to convince followers to join the change process (Dunoon, 2002).

Barbuto, J. E., Jr., & Burbach, M. E. (2006). The emotional intelligence of transformational leaders: A field study of elected officials. *The Journal of Social Psychology, 146,* 51–64. doi:10.3200/SOCP.146.1.51-64

The main purpose of the Barbuto and Burbach (2006) study was to know how leaders can use the transformational model to improve productivity by inspiring workers. The authors' survey indicated that those who practice the transformational model achieve greater success in stimulating employees to do well in their jobs. Barbuto and Burbach also explicated that leaders use the transformational model to persuade workers to embrace their positive visions and ideals to change their organization's direction. The authors' hypothesis strongly supported the idea that the transformational model enables leaders to motivate workers to contribute more to the success of the policy they initiated.

Mizrahi, T., & Berger C. S. (2005). A longitudinal look at social leadership in hospitals: The impact of a changing health care system. *Journal of Health and Social Work, 300,* 155–165. doi:10.1093/hsw/30.2.155

The authors explored how the transformational-leadership model can help social work administrators respond to the changes that are occurring throughout their hospitals. Mizrahi and Berger (2005) concluded that when using the transformational-leadership model, social work administrators are able to accommodate and adjust to their changing workforce. The hypothesis was that social work administrators are able to respond to changes in their organizations by using the transformational model to inspire workers to embrace the change process. The transformational leader places greater emphasis "on inspiring and motivating followers to work toward a common organizational goal that may supersede individual interests" (p. 192). Additionally, in using the transformational-leadership model, leaders master how to persuade subordinates to accomplish any change they have initiated.

Dionne, S., Yammarino, F. J., Atwater, L. E., & Spangler, W. D. (2004). Transformational leadership and team performance. *Journal of Organizational Management, 2,* 177–193. doi: 10.1108/09534810410530601

The authors' research found that those who use the transformational model build confidence in workers by expressing their visions for organizational change. Leaders speak optimistically about the future and provide an exciting image of organizational change. Dionne, Yammarino, Atwater, and Spangler (2004) contended that "although achieving higher levels of individual performance is widely researched in the transformational leader literature... achieving higher levels of team performance has not been as widely researched" (pp. 177–178). However, this research revealed that the transformational-leadership model is instrumental in the improvement of team performance, which eventually leads to the improvement of the organization as well. The authors demonstrated that "transformational leaders are likely to increase group performance in that they are instrumental in overcoming social loafing among group members" (Dionne et al., 2004, p. 178).

Dvir, T., Kass, N., & Shamir, B. (2004). The emotional bond: Vision and organizational commitment among high-tech employees. *Journal of Organizational Change Management, 17,* 126–143. doi:10.1108/09534810410530575

The authors examined how transformational leaders create a vision to generate higher levels of worker commitments to the success of the organization. Dvir, Kass, and Shamir (2004) also supported the notion that leaders use the transformational technique to inspire followers to perform exceptionally well in their jobs. The heart of transformational leadership is focusing attention on a meaningful vision to achieve the objective. The leader's power relies on vision and motivating employees to achieve effective change. The authors argued that, through the transformational model, leaders are able to articulate their visions effectively and change the mind of those who are resistant to change.

Oswick, C., Grant, D., Michelson, G., & Wailes, N. (2005). Looking forwards: Discursive directions in organizational change. *Journal of Organizational Change Management, 18,* 383–390. doi: 10.1108/09534810510607074

The authors' study drew attention to the need of managers to prepare for organizational change and future development. Public managers who fail to embrace change when it is required for future development are likely to fail. The authors reinforce the notion, stating:

> The message to organizations and managers is simple: you live in a rapidly changing world and you have to change rapidly to survive. There is an implicit threat embedded within this message (i.e., failure to embrace change will result in organizational failure). (Oswick, Grant, Michelson, & Wailes, 2005, p. 384)

Organizations will continue to face multiple problems, such as the challenge of providing quality services, increases in competition, and changing customer demands. Managers should be able to adapt and provide new initiatives to transform their organizations to meet changing markets. Training employees and providing them with updated information and new technologies will help meet new changes in the market. The authors explained that in "the hyper turbulent environment of the 21st century, managers are confronting information technology and a chaotic world of changing markets and consumer lifestyles" (p. 383).

Organizations need to be aware of these new technologies, which are instrumental to their development. Oswick et al. (2005) used literature reviews and surveys to research how leaders used new information technologies to simplify work activities and improve an organization's performance. The authors' research findings supported the contention that information technologies have changed the way organizations operate. For instance, different computers are introduced to the market nearly every month.

Iedema, R., Rhodes, C., & Scheeres, H. (2005). Presenting identity: Organizational change and immaterial labor. *Journal of Organizational Management, 18,* 327–337. doi: 10.1108/09534810510607038

The authors' studies supported the contention that organizations have changed remarkably due to the frequent updating of communication and information technologies, which enable people from every area in the organization to work faster and contribute to their work activities in different ways. The authors contended that "technologies are playing a key role in disrupting 'old' demarcations as new alliances and configurations are opened up and made possible, not only between disparate player organizations, but also across organizations nationally and internationally" (Iedema, Rhodes, & Scheeres, 2005, p. 184). Technologies will continue to be the key to work renovation, and managers should take advantage of them to improve their workforce.

Downey, J. (2001). Academic leadership and organizational change. *Journal of Innovative Higher Education, 25,* 235–236. doi: 10.1023/A: 1011090406140

Downey (2001) explored how the transformational model can help academic leaders articulate their visions effectively to improve standards in their institutions. "Part of the challenge for academic leaders is to find ways to capture and articulate elements of that vision for and to their own institution and to do so in ways that enhance standards" with the aid of the transformational-leadership model (Downey, 2001, p. 237). The notion is that the transformational-leadership model should not only be used to focus on improving leaders' skills, but also be used by leaders to articulate their visions, which will enable them to inspire students to achieve higher standards in and outside their institutions. The author reviewed literature to support the contention that the transformational model focuses too much on improving an organization's performance through leadership. To improve students' skills and ideas, leaders can use the transformational-leadership model.

Simonson, M. (2005). Distance education: Eight steps for transforming an organization. *The Quarterly Review of Distance Education, 6*(2), vii–viii.

The author explored how distance-education leaders create a vision to transform their institutions. "A distance education leader is a visionary capable of action who guides an organization's future vision, mission, goals, and objectives." (Simonson, 2005, p. vii). This research supports the argument that distance-education leaders are able to institutionalize the changes they initiated through their visions. This author demonstrated that distance-education leaders use their visions to find a better way to diversify the students' population. In addition, through the vision of leaders, they are able to introduce more compelling instruction and interactive learning styles to the institution.

The idea of the research was that vision is one of the most powerful weapons any distance-education leader possesses. Indeed, research findings supported the notion that leaders use their visions to inspire students to become successful in their careers: leaders in developing a new direction for the institution and students following that direction. Transformation of distance education relies on leaders' visions and their competence to transform the educational system in a way that will greatly impact the lives of students more than those who have been enrolled in traditional institutions.

Treleaven L., & Sykes, C. (2005). Loss of organizational knowledge: From supporting clients to serving head office. *Journal of Organizational Change Management, 18,* 353–368. doi: 10.1108/09534810510607056

The hypothesis of the authors' research was that organizational knowledge is lost during the organizational-change process. Treleaven and Sykes (2005) defined organizational knowledge as the "capability members of an organization have developed to draw distinctions in the process of carrying out their work, in particular concrete contexts, by enacting sets of generalizations whose application depends on historically evolved collective understanding" (p. 356).

Changes in organization procedures result in actions that are different from the knowledge the organization has developed for a period of time. During the change process, some organizational knowledge is eliminated, whereas new knowledge is generated. Treleaven and Sykes (2005) used data and a review of the literature to support the contention that "change dynamically produced by the everyday actions of organization members engaged in their work, dramatically but nevertheless continuously, recreates and replaces organizational knowledge" (p. 356). The research findings supported the hypothesis that organizational knowledge may be lost when tasks are performed by members of the organization during the organizational change.

Yukl, G., Fu, P. P., & McDonald, R. (2003). Cross-cultural differences in perceived effectiveness of influence tactics for initiating or resisting change. *Applied Psychology, 52,* 68–82. doi:10.1111/1464-0597.00124

The authors' research method was based on a questionnaire given to managers from different nations. Yukl, Fu, and McDonald (2003) examined tactics managers from different cultures use in gaining approval for or resisting proposed change initiated by their bosses. The research revealed that the United States and Western managers favor using persuasion and inspiration as a tactic to gain support for or disapproval of the policy changes initiated by their superiors. Managers from China other Eastern nations prefer to use an informal approach, such as seeking third-party help to draw support to the new policies that have been initiated by leaders to change the organizations' direction. "For resisting change, Chinese managers are likely to have a more favorable perception of passive tactics like avoidance and procrastination" (p. 70). Eastern managers are likely to be afraid to disagree with the changes initiated by their leaders or superiors. In contrast, Western managers do not hesitate to point out the weaknesses in their leaders' proposed change. Indeed, this research is instrumental in understanding how managers from different nations address new policies in organizational change.

Morrison, J. (2003). A timely leader strategy for change. *Journal of Education for Business,* 315.

The main purpose of the research was to see how corporate leaders can implement change that is more favorable to the environment rather than to make more profit. Morrison (2003) explored how corporate CEOs can be more sensitive to their environment and workforce. The researcher found that corporate executives can be more socially responsible if they develop a policy that addresses the human aspect of their organizations, showing they care more about their communities' and workers' well-being.

The author demonstrated that "to change the way that business is conducted, corporations may need to establish new operational styles that set new expectations for both today's work force and corporate accountability" (p. 124). CEOs should not be considered as leaders who are only interested in profit, but also as people who care about their workforce and environment. The researcher revealed that the credibility of CEOs in the United States will improve if they develop a policy that addresses environmental and social issues such as workers healthcare, education, human rights, and disposal of toxic waste.

McAlearney, A. S. Fisher, D., Heiser, K., Robbins, D., & Kelleher, K. (2005). Developing effective physician leaders: Changing cultures and transforming organizations. *Hospital Topics, 83*(2), 11–18.

The authors explored how physician leaders can develop entrepreneur skills. Physicians' leadership development is essential because of the current market competition for quality healthcare. McAlearney, Fisher, Heiser, Robbins, and Kelleher (2005) used data analysis and a review of the literature to support the contention that "as the business of medicine become more and more complex, the need for qualified physicians to participate in the leadership of the medical enterprise is keenly experienced by many healthcare organizations" (p. 11). The authors' research encouraged physician leaders to develop entrepreneur and leadership skills to manage health care, which gives them the opportunity to apply new skills in practice.

Most previous studies focused on how physicians managed stress and used risky techniques to save patients' lives. However, very few studies considered how physician leaders could develop entrepreneurial skills to manage resources and the marketing of different medical services to patients. The primary goal of physicians is to care for patients and save lives. Nevertheless, research findings supported the contention that physicians need entrepreneurial skills because they significantly impact the use of healthcare resources and delivery of quality medical care (McAlearney et al., 2005).

Brown, D. A., Humphreys, M., & Gurney, P. M. (2004). Narrative, identity and change: A case study of Laskarina Holidays. *Journal of Organizational Change Management, 18,* 312–326. doi: 10.1108/09534810510607029

The authors examined an organization's identity based on the narratives of the workers at Laskarina Holidays in the United Kingdom. Brown, Humphreys, and Gurney's (2004) research supported the contention that "just as individuals tend to author multiple narratives about themselves, so they will often construct many distinct stories about the organizations in which they participate as owners, employees, customers, partners and shareholders" (p. 314). The notion of an organization identity is how workers see themselves in the organization and what they think the organization stands for. Employees' narratives offer a descriptive historical view of how workers perceive their organizations.

Through the workers' narratives, Brown et al. (2004) were able to identify what workers think about the organization in which they work, whether they are satisfied with their jobs, and how the organization is managed. The interviews of workers at Laskarina' Holidays yielded a majority view of how they perceived the organization. The majority of employees were happy with the organizational identity. This signifies that they were satisfied with the way the organization conducts businesses and the company's treatment of workers. However, some workers were dissatisfied with their working conditions. For instance, "a few staff voiced complaints about how the organization was managed" (p. 319). Some workers suggested leaders should change the way the organization is managed, especially in working conditions of workers. An organization may decide to change its direction based on the moral narratives of workers, responding to how workers view the organization.

References

Barbuto, J. E., Jr., & Burbach, M. E. (2006). The emotional intelligence of transformational leaders: A field study of elected officials. *The Journal of Social Psychology, 146,* 51–64. doi:10.3200/SOCP.146.1.51-64

Bechard, R., & Harris, R. T. (1977). *Organizational transitions: Managing complex change.* Boston, MA: Addison-Wesley.

Brown, D. A., Humphreys, M., & Gurney, P. M. (2004). Narrative, identity and change: A case study of Laskarina Holidays. *Journal of Organizational Change Management, 18,* 312–326. doi: 10.1108/09534810510607029

Daiziel, M., & Schoonver, D. (1988). *Changing ways: A practical tool for implementing change within organizations.* New York, NY: Amacom.

Dean, A. (2001). *Beyond change management: Advanced strategies for today's transformational leaders.* San Francisco, CA: John Wiley & Sons.

Dionne, S., Yammarino, F. J., Atwater, L. E., & Spangler, W. D. (2004). Transformational leadership and team performance. *Journal of Organizational Management, 2,* 177–193. doi: 10.1108/09534810410530601

Downey, J. (2001). Academic leadership and organizational change. *Journal of Innovative Higher Education, 25,* 235–236. doi:10.1023/A: 1011090406140

Dunoon D. (2002). Rethinking leadership for the public sector. *Australian Journal of Public Administration, 61*(3), 3–18. doi:10.1111/1467-8500.00280

Dvir, T., Kass, N., & Shamir, B. (2004). The emotional bond: Vision and organizational commitment among high-tech employees. *Journal of Organizational Change Management, 17,* 126–143. doi: 10.1108/09534810410530575

Gergen, D., & Kellerman B. (2003). Public leaders: Riding a new tiger. In J. D. Donahue and J. S. Nye, Jr. (Eds.), *For the people: Can we fix public service?* (pp. 13–25). Washington, DC: Brookings Institution.

Gomolski, B. (2000). Change management: Is it the right remedy for e-business growing pain? *InfoWorld, 22*(49), 98.

Hacker, M. E., & Washington, M. (2003). Project leadership and organizational change. *Proceedings of the Institute of Industrial Engineers 19ᵗʰ Annual Conference,* 1–6.

Iedema, R., Rhodes, C., & Scheeres, H. (2005). Presenting identity: Organizational change and immaterial labor. *Journal of Organizational Management, 18,* 327–337. doi: 10.1108/09534810510607038

Johnson E. C. (2005). *Meeting the ethical challenge of leadership: Casting light or shadow* (2ⁿᵈ ed.). Thousand Oaks, CA: Sage.

Kirkpatrick, D. L. (1985). *How to manage change effectively.* San Francisco, CA: Jossey-Bass.

Lipsky, M. (1980). *Street-level bureaucracy: Dilemmas of the public services.* New York, NY: Russell Sage Foundation.

McAlearney, A. S. Fisher, D., Heiser, K., Robbins, D., & Kelleher, K. (2005). Developing effective physician leaders: Changing cultures and transforming organizations. *Hospital Topics, 83*(2), 11–18.

Milakovich, M. E., & Gordon, G. J. (2001). *Public administration in America* (7ᵗʰ ed.). Boston, MA: Bedford/St. Martin's.

Mises, L. V. (1944). *Bureaucracy.* New Haven, CT: Yale University Press.

Mizrahi, T., & Berger C. S. (2005). A longitudinal look at social leadership in hospitals: The impact of a changing health care system. *Journal of Health and Social Work, 300,* 155–165. doi:10.1093/hsw/30.2.155

Morrison, J. (2003). A timely leader strategy for change. *Journal of Education for Business, 315.*

Oswick, C., Grant, D., Michelson, G., &Wailes, N. (2005). Looking forwards: Discursive directions in organizational change. *Journal of Organizational Change Management, 18,* 383–390. doi: 10.1108/09534810510607074

Paul, M. F. (1982). Power, leadership, and trust: Implications for counselors in terms of organizational change. *The Personnel and Guidance Journal, 60*, 538–541. doi: 10.1002/j.2164-4918.1982.tb00716.x

Pillai, R., & Williams, E. A. (2004). Transformational leadership, self-efficacy, group cohesiveness, commitment, and performance. *Journal of Organizational Change Management, 17*, 144–159. doi: 10.1108/09534810410530584

Robbins, S. P. (1987). Organization theory: Structure, design, and applications (2nd ed.). Englewood Cliffs, NJ: Prentice-Hall.

Shafritz, J. M., & Russell, E. W. (2005). *Introducing public administration* (4th ed.). New York, NY: Pearson Education.

Simonson, M. (2005). Distance education: Eight steps for transforming an organization. *The Quarterly Review of Distance Education, 6(2)*, vii–viii.

Steers, M. R. (1991). *Introduction to organizational behavior* (4th ed.). New York, NY: HarperCollins.

Treleaven L., & Sykes, C. (2005). Loss of organizational knowledge: From supporting clients to serving head office. *Journal of Organizational Change Management, 18*, 353–368. doi: 10.1108/09534810510607056

Wilson, J. Q. (1989). *Bureaucracy: What government agencies do and why the do it.* New York, NY: Basic Books.

Yukl, G., Fu, P. P., & McDonald, R. (2003). Cross-cultural differences in perceived effectiveness of influence tactics for initiating or resisting change. *Applied Psychology, 52*, 68–82. doi:10.1111/1464-0597.00124

CHAPTER 3

APPLICATION COMPONENT

Introduction

Bureaucratic principles have dominated U.S. public organizations for many years. Indeed, government policies have been implemented through the bureaucratic hierarchical system (Mises, 1944). Government organizations, such as health, education, and social services rely on the bureaucratic system to manage their organizations. Those systems would have difficulty in recommending dismantling of the bureaucratic system, even though most experts agree that the system is ineffective. Legislative members and clients have criticized the poor delivery of services throughout most social service and other governmental organizations in the United States. Therefore, this chapter seeks to explore how public organization leaders can address bureaucracy and achieve efficiency in delivering services. In addition, the chapter focuses on how the bureaucratic system affects leaders who run social service organizations, such as social-welfare agencies. By knowing the source of the problems of public bureaucracy, recommendations can be made to rectify them.

Traditional bureaucracies have caused many hindrances to the effective development of public organizations (Wilson, 2000). As a result, the new government model should focus on correcting problems and obstacles that come with traditional bureaucracy, such as poor delivery of services, slowness, and lack of resources, flexibility, and innovation (Kamarck, 2003). Workers dislike bureaucracies because of the rules and regulations they must follow to perform their duties. Most workers are willing to do their jobs to the best of their abilities. They want to service their clients better, but bureaucratic hindrances make their efforts ineffective. Public employees harbor much resentment regarding the bureaucratic system. Public bureaucracy causes confusion among workers and makes their jobs difficult. In addition, public employees are compelled to handle multiple tasks with inadequate resources and an inadequate workforce (Wilson, 2000). For example, New York City public school teachers complained about staff reductions, lack of resources, and increased responsibilities. Lipsky (1980) illustrated this position:

> I have never been quite sure what ("increased productivity") means exactly. However, if it means what I think it means, they would like to see us work harder than we ever did before. If this is so, then all proponents of "increased productivity" will be delighted to know that we are doing remarkably well in that department. For example, we have official classes of 45 or more youngsters and minutes in which to take attendance, read circulars, distribute notices, make reports (in duplicate yet), answer questions, etc. In many cases, we have classes, which have rosters of 49 or more children with 30 chairs in the room, or typing classes of 47 with 32 typewriters. Add to this emergency coverage of classes, cafeteria patrol or other building assignments, program, shortage of supplies and equipment and much more—all of this with reduced staff— not to mention the mounds of work we take home with us. The pressures under which we work can never be understood by any productivity, but in so doing we have decreased our effectiveness as human beings to our students, our families and ourselves. (p. 176)

Public defenders have similar problems. Legal aid lawyers are unable to represent clients effectively because of large caseloads assigned to them. Sometimes they come to court without preparing clients' documents or properly interviewing them before the court session. Legal aid lawyers are responsible for 80 to 100 clients. They may be assigned additional clients if there is no one to represent them (Lipsky, 1980). Street-level bureaucracies are usually asking to accept additional tasks, rather than to improve in activities that were already assigned to them. Indeed, public employees are unable to perform their jobs effectively because of large caseloads and bureaucracy in public management (Lipsky, 1980).

Public Bureaucracy and Social Service Organizations

Caseworkers employed by social welfare agencies often complain about the bureaucracy in determining applicants' eligibility for public assistance. They argue that management change procedures nearly every week, which makes it difficult for them to know which are the actual policies and procedures to follow. Katz and Danet (1973) supported the position that caseworkers often lament the bureaucratic restraints under which they have to operate. "Many of them felt that the agency's emphasis on following procedures, and particularly the requirement to investigate closely each recipient's eligibility, make it impossible for them to provide the kind of casework services that would benefit clients most" (pp. 230–231).

In addition, because of the frequent change of policies and procedures, caseworkers are unable to master most jobs. Katz and Danet (1973) supported the notion that new employees find it difficult to master agency procedures; even the old ones were overwhelmed by the complexity of duties. Workers who were unable to understand new policies left the agency unsatisfied. Some did not finish their probation period before they were discharged from the agency. What is more important is that it takes 6 to 12 months to replace employees who are fired or who resigned from the city social services agency. As a result, a higher number of employees are absent or leave every city social services agency. This turnover is quite critical because public-welfare managers rely on workers to perform their jobs and achieve the organization's goals. Lipsky (1980) revealed that "when workers are not replaced their responsibilities are distributed among those who remain, usually without reducing responsibilities they already have" (p. 176). Workers find it quite difficult to catch up with their activities. Consequently, workers do not come to work regularly because they are afraid too much work will be assigned to them. As a result, productivity and efficiency suffer in the workforce.

One can also argue that social-welfare agencies are inefficient because managers focus on reinforcing governmental laws and regulations. They are more worried about complying with laws and policies passed by legislatures, courts, or chief executives than about managing their organizations. As a result, manages spend less time planning how to manage workers' caseloads to provide quality services to clients. Although social-welfare agencies are part of the state chief executive branch, state legislatures have significant power over how public managers operate public-assistance agencies. Ginsberg (1983) demonstrated:

> It is the legislature, which used to determine the level and content for most welfare budgets, passes legislation affecting the authority and responsibility of the agency and in some states determines the levels of cash assistances grants, the scope of the medical care program, the size of the agency's staff, and the salaries paid to public welfare employees. (p. 163)

The actual operations of delivery of services are the responsibility of the public-welfare managers in various cities and counties. Public-welfare managers in various agencies must carry out the policies of the legislature or chief executives. They have no authority to introduce new policies to manage their organizations, apart from ones passed by the legislature or chief executive.

Federal or state governments often introduce new policies and welfare managers are obligated to implement them. When new policies are introduced, sometimes they require more workers to carry out the policies. Managers are unlikely to demand more resources to perform their tasks. They hesitate to do so because of the policies involved. In fact, it takes a significant amount of time for policy makers to approve additional funds for public agencies' new programs.

Another problem is that personnel and civil laws make it very difficult for social-welfare-agency managers to hire more workers to comply with government regulations. Leaders' inability to hire new workers makes it difficult for them to implement the new policy effectively. Public-organization leaders are bound to implement new policies even though they increase workers' caseloads. Indeed, they have to carry out government's policies with fewer resources to do the job. The common strategy among directors is using few workers to perform a task that requires a significant number of workers to do. This strategy has been ineffective, because it leads to higher absenteeism and high turnover.

Moreover, welfare-agency leaders are quite reluctant to use alternative strategies to accomplish agency goals. The argument is that it is the workers' responsibilities to do their jobs, no matter the difficulty. One may say, "I am the manager; my duty as a manager is to make workers do their jobs." The responsibility of a director should be more than to make workers perform their duties. A leader must ensure the agency has enough resources and staff to carry out each particular task. Leaders should be able to think critically and provide ideas on how to achieve goals without overwhelming the workers under their control.

Lacking among managers is concern for workers by caring for their well-being. Caring is quite significant because some caseworkers are not committed to agency rules and procedures due to low morale. Caseworkers may feel that their leaders have no regard for their well- being. In this regard, leaders must learn how to give credit to workers for doing their jobs well. In support of this notion, a regional director of a welfare agency addressed one of the center's staff members: your director has done a tremendous job for reducing the number of people on public assistance. In fact, he has done a wonderful job helping public-assistance recipients move from welfare to work. As a result, some workers were annoyed and walked out of the meeting. They complained that center managers do not find client jobs; they do. Since this incident, the work ethics of some of the workers have slowed down. They hesitated to work overtime, and have stopped volunteering to work during their lunch hours. Sometimes it is necessary to give credit to every worker, even to those who do not merit them. This is significant to boost the morale of workers. It makes them work harder and more energetically to contribute to the success of the organization. Moreover, welfare-agency leaders have not been very successful in executing the agency's policies. One reason is that some policies that have been introduced to reform the welfare agency failed to materialize, due to the complexity of public policy laws and bureaucracy. In addition, workers were not properly trained on the new policies. As a result, most of the new policies were ineffective.

One common problem in most welfare agencies is that too much time is devoted to training. Too much time is assigned to workers' training and meetings. More importantly, training programs are ineffective. Workers find it difficult to apply what they have learned in training to their actual jobs. Most training is about policies and directives. The training programs do not simplify work activities or implement effective ways for workers to perform their jobs. In addition, the training programs do not focus on how to reduce red tape or bureaucracy; neither have they addressed how workers' job performance can be improved.

The hierarchy system makes it very difficult for caseworkers to process applications in a timely manner. Katz and Danet (1973) supported the argument that caseworkers lament bureaucracy that they are compelled to follow to perform their jobs.

> They always talk about social work, but actually you can't do anything of the kind here. For instance, I had one case, which I wanted to send to another agency, but my supervisor said, "you can't. You would have to make a case plan first, and we can't do that." (p. 231)

The system is heavy with too many procedures, policies that are not clearly defined and confused workers. Additionally, a case is not complete until office managers and a supervisor approve it. In some cases, a deputy director must approve a case, and then forward it to an office manager and a supervisor to sign before clients receive benefits. Indeed, the bureaucracy in social-welfare procedures causes many obstacles to workers' effective delivery of services. For workers to get their work done, they are forced to jump around the bureaucracy (Behn, 2003).

Decision-Making Power and Public-Organization Leaders

Public-organization leaders face a major obstacle to reform the system. Although been several policies were implemented to reform public organizations, they have not materialized. Behn (2003) explicated, "Little wonder that the governmental landscape is letter with discarded reforms: the planning, program, budgeting system; management by objective; Zero-Based Budgeting; Total Quality management. Each was design to force fundamental change, to require public agencies to improve performance" (p. 192). One reason public-organization reform fails is that leaders have no decision-making power. They have no authority to introduce their own policies to improve the agency's performance. For instance, at a welfare-agency staff meeting, a staff member complained to one of the center directors that caseworkers have no basic material to perform their jobs. Some broken computers have not been repaired for more than 2 months. In addition, too many vacant positions remained. The director's answer was that his responsibility was to inform the regional director about the complaints, and the steps needed to rectify the problems. The regional director has no power to instruct the personnel office to hire more workers or purchase new computers, and cannot instruct the technician to repair the computers. Based on procedures and policies, directors must inform the regional director about the shortage of workers, and the regional center would inform the commissioner's office. However, the commissioner cannot instruct the personnel office to hire new workers unless there are sufficient funds in the authorized budget. In some cases, the commissioner has to notify the mayor or the city council to get additional funds to hire new workers. Once again, the problem facing public organizations is that leaders have no access to funds and power to make decisions to hire or fire workers. In addition, public managers are not allowed to introduce their own policies or laws to reform the bureaucracy. Many welfare-agency directors complain that services are slow because of government policies that govern public organizations. They argue forcefully that civil service laws weaken their power to make decisions to implement the reforms they need. In addition, in most cases, they focus on implementing new government policies. They are more concerned about complying with government laws, rather than developing ideas to improve services to clients.

One key characteristic is that a leader must have rational skills, supported by sound decision-making skills. However, in public organizations owned by governments, the decisions-making authority no longer resides with the leader; simply, a leader is not even a leader in a governmental organization, but rather is a mere pauper. This status not only impacts negatively on the leader, but also on team members, as all feel demotivated and even at times powerless. This sense of being enslaved has a negative effect on their productivity and finally causes a substantial loss to the organization as well. Here, simply, the government must consider their demands and needs, and must keep their wants and need a priority.

Even if government wants to implement their decisions, they must appoint their own people in charge; however, they must train them in such a way that they develop a sense of servant leadership. Greenleaf coined the term servant leadership, suggesting that such leaders must sacrifice their own wants and needs for their team members. If the appointed body is a servant leader, the leader must then attribute to the government's wants and needs, along with those of organizational members, a priority. If the leader does so, the organization will maintain positive revenues—a goal of government—but also experience significant increases in employee and team motivation.

If public managers continue to spend too much time planning and implementing government policies, the reform of public organizations is unlikely to materialize. However, it is unnecessary to wait for policymakers to reform public organizations, because managers can do it. Public leaders will be able to implement the reform public managers' needs, if they are given the necessary tools and labor. Behn (2003) supported the argument:

> {The}... strategy is to fix the managers—help them develop the leadership capacity necessary to procedure results.... Rather than reformulate the systems of government to conform to some administrative ideals, we ought to help our public managers

to function effectively given the restrictions and opportunities created by those systems. (p. 192)

Public managers lack political support and resources to carry out their duties. Therefore, it is important that they are encouraged to continue to work in public organizations. In addition, public-organization leaders as well as their workers are underpaid. They face greater criticisms from the public and policy makers than their counterparts in nonprofit and private organizations. In fact, public managers should be commended because it is a very difficult task to manage public organizations. This difficulty ensues because public managers must address multiple tasks and a large population of people.

Despite the several obstacles public leaders face, they must also be able to develop new government models that are effective enough to reduce public bureaucracy. The new model must be supported and authorized by the mayor and city council. Public-organization leaders must be good administrators with public policy savvy to persuade unions, city council members, and the mayor to give them the authority to reform public bureaucracy. The new government model departs from the culture of public leaders who sit at the top of the hierarchy and direct workers to perform tasks. Public leaders can be administrators and simultaneously be involved in public policy, so they can negotiate with policymakers to give them the power to oversee their organizations.

A few years ago, New York City public-school managers were known for their bureaucratic waste and ineffective management. The New York City public school board was dismantled by the city council after the city's mayor, Michael Bloomberg, demanded the power to run the city public schools. As a result, the mayor was able to implement some new policies, which led to effective reform of public school management. One policy the mayor implemented was having the public school board report directly to him.

In fact, public leaders' ideas and actions are irrelevant unless lawmakers and governmental laws support them. In New Zealand, lawmakers have given their public managers power similar to that of managers in the private sector. Public managers have the authority to design policies and implement them. In addition, they have the power to fire and hire workers. Kamarck (2003) explained, "Public managers in New Zealand have more control over their budgets, personnel, and other management systems and can be fired at will" (p.137). New Zealand public mangers are more effective than U.S. leaders because they have decision-making power.

Indeed, the bureaucratic system will remain Ineffective without public-organization leaders with the authority to reform the system. Therefore, public leaders must demand decision-making power from lawmakers. Public managers will gain this power if leaders of various public organizations request the authority to make decisions to reform public bureaucracy.

Public-organization leader' solutions are central to the key reform of public management. Behn (2003) elucidated, "As we seek to improve public service, we are in danger of ignoring the necessity of improving the capacity of public managers to lead their agencies" (p. 191). Public-organization leaders should have the will and philosophy to convince policymakers that they need the decision-making power to service the public better. Without this power, policymakers will continue to undermine public-organization leaders' power and ideas to run their organizations. Consequently, giving public-organization leaders the authority to make decisions to reform their organizations will enable policymakers to hold them accountable for their actions. Public leaders will no longer have the excuse that their hands are tied and they do not have the power to run their organizations. What is important is that they will be able to introduce ideas and policies to reduce bureaucracy and waste in public management.

Bureaucracy and the Personnel System

Public-organization leaders face great problems recruiting qualified candidates because of bureaucracy in the personnel system. Public-organization' personnel systems are bureaucratic and tedious. Bilmes and Neal (2003) illustrated that it takes government personnel an average of 82 days to make a hiring decision. Even when candidates are accepted, it takes an average of 3 months to process their applications. In addition, the

Office of Management and Budget must review all accepted candidates' applications before making final decisions. More important, the rules and regulations in the government personnel system make it difficult for job applicants outside government agencies to be employed (Anechiarico & Jacobs, 1996).

Additionally, government personnel systems have been manipulated to allow people who work in public organizations to gain promotions or find employment. Undoubtedly, nepotism and favoritism are just a few hindrances quality candidates face when trying to gain employment in government organizations. This contention can be verified that in some government job vacancies were already filled before they were published on the Internet. It is unethical that a candidate was discouraged by the city agency personnel official that the job he intended to apply for was already occupied, before it was publish.

Even federal government job vacancies are systematically designed for candidates who are already employed by the agency to fill vacant positions. Bilmes and Neal (2003) supported the argument that some federal government jobs are barely open to outside applicants. They also reinforced the contention that some federal jobs were offered to applicants who the recruiter knew: "Many positions are essentially rigged; and the hiring manager has a candidate in mind before staring the recruitment process" (p. 116).

Indeed, the deficiency in the government personnel system is one of the obstacles to effective management of public organizations. The most effective management takes place when a leader is able to employ well-qualified people and put the best team in place to achieve the organization's goals (Gergen & Kellerman, 2003). Without this ability, a marked possibility of slowness in delivering services and waste of organizational resources will ensue. Therefore, it is important to have flexibility in the public personnel system. Personnel officials should not be allowed to make all employment decisions. Leaders should have some authority in deciding who should be hired or fired.

Recommendations

For social-welfare agencies to achieve their goals, leaders must be able to empower workers and provide ideas and detailed plans about how the agency should function. Employee training is meaningful. Training programs should address how workers can manage caseloads and provide effective services to clients. Workers must be able to apply what they have learned in training to their actual jobs.

Hence, the organization must always place their members, who would act as a liaison between them to create the perfect profitable bridge between organizational goals and profitability. In addition, organizations could increase employee salaries and try to listen to employees more often. Furthermore, they must train their appointees to be better leaders who will place organizational vision and employee needs before their own and hence guide the organization to the desired success, reaching such heights of innovation and achievement not previously realized.

Another suggestion for the reform of public management is that new public leaders should have Master of Public Administration and Political science degrees, preferably a doctorate in Political Science/Public Policy and Administration, and law degrees. In addition, they should have some experience in public management. Thus, new public leaders will have the necessary skills and education to bargain with policymakers and union leaders to seek more funds to operate their organizations.

This ability to negotiate is quite essential because public management involves complex government policies and laws that new leaders must comprehend. Kobrak (2002) reinforced the notion that leadership training is necessary "because the legislative branch gives public agencies missions that are vague and conflicting and fails to provide enough resources to pursue seriously all of these missions" (p. 50). Consequently, public organizations should set up a center for leadership development. This center will serve as a place where all public leaders are trained on how to interpret and implement government policies. Training will also help public leaders develop strategic plans to reduce bureaucracy in management and use resources to achieve goals. Policymakers should be educated on the necessity to give greater authority to public administrators to operate their organizations. This policy motion can be made in community forums or public administration conferences attended by public managers to discuss strategies to convince policymakers that to have effective reform, it is essential to give public managers more authority to run their organizations.

Conclusion

I identified the problems of public bureaucracies. The bureaucratic system is slow; it has poor service delivery and lacks innovation. Current research and breadth and depth components have pointed out that the bureaucracy in the public-management system causes many hindrances to effective production. Many experts, policymakers, and the public as well have complained bitterly about their dissatisfaction with public bureaucracy. Behn (2003) wrote,

> The curse word bureaucracy is so associated with government that the phrase government bureaucracy is considered redundant.... Every citizen can tell a horror story about his, her, or a friend's personal interaction with a public bureaucracy—be that a municipal school, a state driver's license bureau, or a federal regulatory agency. (p. 193)

In business plans, marketing managers focus on the application of marketing techniques, the firm's management techniques, and managing the resources and activities. The scope of the marketing relies on the size of the business and its goals. One researcher (Jackson, 1983) reinforced the notion that clients provided inadequate services often criticize public employees: "the rules... of bureaucrats frequently frustrate clients who complain that simple requests are dealt with in a complex manner; they argued that procedures are stupid, because they are forced to waste time dealing with the bureaucracy" (Jackson, 1983, p. 7).

In fact, not bureaucrats, but the governmental policies and multiple administrative procedures they are obliged to follow (Francis & Stone, 1956) are the main cause of the inefficiency of public services. Bureaucrats will be able to provide adequate services to clients if the bureaucracy in public management is reduced. Gergen and Kellerman (2003) supported the argument that the hierarchical system in public management should be restructured whereby lower level workers will be able to make decisions without going through the people at the top: "Power must be allowed to move down within organizations, so that those at lower levels can act quickly on their own, unhampered by bureaucratic rigidities" (Gergen & Kellerman, 2003, p. 14). For example, waiting time for people applying for welfare benefits can be reduced from 60 to 39 minutes if lower level workers are allowed to make certain decisions that enable them to provide faster service to clients.

Gergen and Kellerman (2003) contended that public leaders should not try to be micromanagers. Rather, they should focus on developing ideas how workers can service clients fastest. Gergen and Kellerman also argued "that is not to say that the person at the top must hand all decision making to others below; that person must still set a direction, determine goals, and mobilize others" (p. 14). Additionally, leaders should not always be the people who sit at the top to make decisions; rather, they must ensure the organization has sufficient resources to implement policies and the organizations' intended purpose is well served.

Another reason public-organization leaders have not been able to provide quality services to clients is that they have no decision-making power. Public leaders must implement government policies even though they disagree with them. In fact, they are not allowed to set policies for their organizations like private-sector leaders because of governmental laws. Wilson (1989) illustrated: "In principle the legislature could allow the Social Security Administration, the Defense Department, or the New York City school system to follow the same rules as IBM, General Electric, or Harvard University" (p. 20). In practice, public-organization leaders are not allowed to operate like those in the private sector because of the politics involved. Government laws and policies can change if it is necessary to make the workforce efficient. As a result, public-organization leaders need decision-making power to set their own policies, because that power is central to effective management. If public leaders have the power to make decisions to run their organizations, they will be able to introduce reforms, enabling them to compete with private-sector leaders in service delivery.

As stated in the depth-component research findings, one reform in public management is allowing public managers to have the power to negotiate with policymakers, which gives them the right to offer rewards to workers who perform exceptionally well. Public leaders also can introduce policies that will allow employees to be promoted and get higher salaries based on performance. Consequently, the performance of workers will improve and the organization will be able to attract outside candidates to seek employment in the agency. Behn (2003) reinforced the idea:

> Public agencies would pay their employees according to their performance. Then these agencies would motivate all their employees to produces real results (encouraging the high performers to remain in government (and work even harder and smarter, while also prompting the low performers to leave). (p. 193)

This idea is worth trying, because for a long time, private organizations have been using pay-for-performance strategies to drive production (Borjas, 2003). Research described in the breadth component revealed that performance data is essential to the improvement of public management. In fact, performance data helps leaders know what they are doing right and wrong. Through performance, leaders can develop feedback that will enable them to set their organizations on the right path. Most importantly, performance data helps leaders correct errors and enables leaders to monitor work progress and achieve projected outcomes (Behn, 2004).

Additionally, for public-organization leaders to achieve good results, the personnel-management system should be reformed. The public-organization employment system is slow and ineffective. Bureaucracy in the public-organization personnel system and civil laws make it very difficult to hire new workers in a timely fashion. As a result, the hiring and firing process in the public personnel system should be restructured to enable vacant positions to be filled when needed. This new structure will help in employing more qualified candidates from outside public agencies. This change is quite significant because it gives public leaders the opportunity to have more qualified workers who are capable of performing tasks effectively. The best leaders are those who are able to assemble the best team of workers to perform tasks (Gergen & Kellerman, 2003). Therefore, public-organization leaders should have some authority to choose their teams and employ capable workers to achieve their goals.

References

Anechiarico, F., & Jacobs, B. J. (1996). *The pursuit of absolute integrity.* Chicago, IL: The University of Chicago Press.

Behn, R. D. (2003). *Creating leadership capacity for the twenty-first century: Not another technical fix.* Washington, DC: Brookings Institution.

Behn, R. D. (2004). *Performance leadership: 11 better practices that can ratchet up performance.* Cambridge, MA: Harvard University John F. Kennedy of School of Government.

Bilmes, L., & Neal, R. J. (2003). *The people factor: Human resources reform in government.* Washington, DC: Brookings Institution.

Borjas, G. J. (2003). *Wage structures and the sorting of workers into the public sector.* Washington, DC: Brookings Institution.

Francis, R. G., & Stone, R. C. (1956). *Service and procedure in bureaucracy.* Minneapolis: The University of Minnesota Press.

Gergen, D., & Kellerman B. (2003). Public leaders: Riding a new tiger. In J. D. Donahue and J. S. Nye, Jr. (Eds.), *For the people: Can we fix public service?* (pp. 13–25). Washington, DC: Brookings Institution.

Ginsberg, L. H. (1983). *The practice of social work in public welfare.* New York, NY: The Free Press.

Jackson, P. M. (1983). *The political economy of bureaucracy.* Totowa, NJ: RI

Kamarck, E. C. (2003). *Public servants for twenty-first-century government.* Washington, DC: Brookings Institution.

Katz, E., & Danet, B. (1973). *Bureaucracy and the public.* New York, NY: Basic Books.

Kobrak, P. (2002). *The political environment of public management.* New York, NY: Longman

Lipsky, M. (1980). *Street-level bureaucracy: Dilemmas of the individuals in public services.* New York: Russell Sage Foundation.

Mises, L. V. (1944). *Bureaucracy.* New Haven, CT: Yale University Press.

Wilson J. Q. (1989). *Bureaucracy: What government agencies do and why they do it.* New York, NY: Basic Books.

GLOSSARY

Buyers: Those who carry out the formal arrangements for purchase, service, delivery, and financial terms.

Compensatory-decision rule: A type of decision rule for evaluating alternatives where consumers consider each brand with respect to how it performs on relevant or salient attributes and the importance of each attribute. This decision rule allows for a negative evaluation or performance on a particular attribute to be compensated for by a positive evaluation on another attribute.

Compensatory model: A model that assumes consumers judge a limited number of product attributes, that the attributes vary in importance to the consumer, and that strength in one area compensates for weakness in another.

Competitive advantage: The part of a firm's total offering that is superior to that of its competitors.

Competitors: Something unique or special that a firm does or possesses that provides an advantage over its competitors.

Consumer markets: The most visible markets, which consist of individual customers who buy products for their own use or for use by other members of their households.

Core benefit: The need that a product fulfills or the problem it solves.

Customer satisfaction: The extent to which a product's perceived performance matches a buyer's expectations. If the product's performance falls short of expectations, the buyer is dissatisfied. If performance matches or exceeds expectations, the buyer is satisfied or delighted.

Demand: A relationship among the various amounts of a product that buyers would be willing and able to purchase at possible alternative prices during a given period of time, all other factors remaining the same.

Demands: Human wants that are backed by buying power.

De-marketing: Marketing to reduce demand temporarily or permanently; the aim is not to destroy demand, but only to reduce or shift it.

Horizontal markets: Markets on which products are sold to a wide range of industries.

Market: The set of all actual and potential buyers of a product or service.

Marketing: A social managerial process whereby individuals and groups obtain what they need and want by creating and exchanging products and value with others.

Marketing concept: The philosophy that business organizations achieve their profit and other goals by satisfying consumers.

Marketing environment: The actors and forces outside marketing that affect marketing management's ability to develop and maintain successful transactions with target customers.

Marketing-information system: People, equipment, and procedures to gather, sort, analyze, evaluate, and distribute needed, timely, and accurate information to marketing decision makers.

Marketing intelligence: Everyday information about developments in the marketing environment that helps manager prepares and adjusts marketing plans.

Marketing management: The analysis, planning, implementation, and control of programs designed to create, build, and maintain beneficial exchanges with target buyers to achieving organizational objectives.

Marketing research: The systematic design, collection, analysis, and reporting of data relevant to a specific marketing situation facing an organization.

Non-compensatory model: A model of information processing in which a high rating for one attribute does not offset a low rating for other.

Product: Anything that can be offered to a market for attention, acquisition, use, or consumption that might satisfy a want or need. Products include physical objects, services, persons, places, organizations, and ideas.

Service: Any activity or benefit that one party can offer to another that is essentially intangible and does not result in the ownership of anything.

Service market: All organizations that buy in order to produce services.

Social marketing (or cause marketing): The design, implementation, and control of marketing programs calculated to influence the acceptability of social ideas.

THE AUTHOR

Dr. Napoleon Imarhiagbe was born in Edo State in Nigeria. For the past twenty two years, he resided in New York City in the United States of America. Dr. Imarhiagbe is an expert in public management and a trained administrator. He has a bachelor degree in Public Administration from Medgar Evers of the City University of New York (CUNY). He earned a Master of Public Administration (MPA) from John Jay College of Criminal Justice (CUNY) with a specialization in Management and Operations. He graduated with distinction from the prestigious Walden University School of public Management with a Ph.D. in Public Policy and Administration. Dr. Imarhiagbe has participated in numerous studies and program developments including his contribution to the development of the Medgar Evers College Census Information Center. Most of his published articles are on public management. In 2002, Dr. Imarhiagbe was awarded the National Dean's list Honoring America's Outstanding Student. Dr. Imarhiagbe also received the Strathmore Who's Who 2015 award.

The knowledge and experience he brings to this study is his 14 years of experience working with the New York City Department of Social Services. This experience enables him to understand how public organizations work. It also enables him to understand that good leadership skills and work ethics are just a few factors that continue to improve public management.

www.ingramcontent.com/pod-product-compliance
Lightning Source LLC
Chambersburg PA
CBHW030909180526
45163CB00004B/1768